EASY TEXTURED
KNITS

By Margret Willson

LEISURE ARTS, INC.
Little Rock, Arkansas

EDITORIAL STAFF
Vice President and Editor-in-Chief:
  Susan White Sullivan
Knit and Crochet Publications Director:
  Lindsay White Glenn
Special Projects Director: Susan Frantz Wiles
Senior Prepress Director: Mark Hawkins
Art Publications Director: Rhonda Shelby
Technical Writer: Lois J. Long
Technical Editors: Linda Daley, Sarah J. Green,
  and Cathy Hardy
Editorial Writer: Susan McManus Johnson
Art Category Manager: Lora Puls
Graphic Artists: Katherine Laughlin, Becca Snider
  and Dana Vaughn
Imaging Technician: Stephanie Johnson
Prepress Technician: Janie Marie Wright
Photography Manager: Katherine Laughlin
Contributing Photographers: Jason Masters,
  Mark Mathews, and Ken West
Contributing Photo Stylists: Angela Alexander,
  Sondra Daniel, Brooke Duszota, and
  Christy Myers
Publishing Systems Administrator: Becky Riddle
Mac Information Technology Specialist:
  Robert Young

BUSINESS STAFF
President and Chief Executive Officer:
  Rick Barton
Vice President of Sales: Mike Behar
Director of Finance and Administration:
  Laticia Mull Dittrich
Director of Corporate Planning: Anne Martin
National Sales Director: Martha Adams
Creative Services: Chaska Lucas
Information Technology Director: Hermine Linz
Controller: Francis Caple
Vice President, Operations: Jim Dittrich
Retail Customer Service Manager: Stan Raynor
Print Production Manager: Fred F. Pruss

Library of Congress Control Number: 2011938744

ISBN-13: 978-1-60900-336-4

TABLE OF CONTENTS

The world of knitting is a magical place filled with learning and discovery.

Textured Knitting requires only the simplest of skills and only a little more attention than plain knitting. Whether you are a beginning knitter who's ready for the next step, or an accomplished knitter seeking a fascinating interlude, textured knitting is for you. If you can cast on and bind off, knit and purl, you can make the majority of the projects in this book. Add a basic increase and decrease, and you can make them all!

You will find that textured knitting is a scenic byway across the landscapes of fabric you create. Adventure awaits you at every turn as you learn new stitch combinations. Although the fabrics consist only of knit and purl, they each have a character of their own. Getting to know them is like making new friends!

May your world be filled with knitting, and your knitting filled with joy.

—Margret

ABOUT THE DESIGNER

Margret Willson's lovely designs are known for their accuracy and innovation. As Margret says, "I am always thinking of the person who might follow the pattern I have written. Is it clear and concise? Is it easy to follow? Beyond pleasing the editor, one must think of the stitchers. Are they likely to be frustrated by the pattern? Will they be pleased with the result? Now, more and more, I add to that list of questions, 'Is it fun?' No matter how beautiful the design looks in the photograph, if I haven't done my job as a pattern writer and enabled the person following the pattern to replicate the design, AND enjoy doing so, I have failed miserably."

This philosophy is one that has served Margret and her readers very well, supplying them all with the enjoyment of creating excellent knitwear and accessories. Margret lives near Salt Lake City, Utah and finds inspiration in her surroundings. "I love the mountains, but I also have access to libraries, yarn shops, and anything else I need. I keep a room for my work, but it often follows me through the house and out to the front porch. I stitch my own models, which gives me the freedom to make changes as I go."

Knitting represents more than a vocation to Margret. It is a personal joy, one she learned from her talented and generous grandmother.

Margret has created dozens of designs for a popular yarn company and dozens more have appeared in magazines and pattern collections. To see a wide selection of these projects, look for Margret's listing as MWillsonDesigns at Ravelry.com and visit her blog at MargretsMusings.blogspot.com.

ABOUT THIS BOOK

The purpose of this book is to share a collection of the countless fabrics that can be created with only knit and purl, and to give you the inspiration and confidence to enjoy using them.

At the heart of *Easy Textured Knits* is the Stitch Gallery. Gathered for you are 72 stitch patterns complete with photos, row-by-row instructions and charts. Whether you work through the book from beginning to end (projects are organized in order of difficulty, with the easiest first), find a stitch pattern and choose something to make with it, or find a project and go back to practice the stitches—the choice is up to you!

In any case, the best place to begin is with Understanding Stitch Multiples and Charts, page 6. This is recommended even if stitch patterns are not new to you, since there are a few conventions used in this book which may be unfamiliar. The General Instructions contain a refresher course on the basics of knitting, an explanation of abbreviations used in this book, and helpful yarn, skill, and needle charts.

MATERIALS NEEDED

Each project will list materials specific to that project.

What follows is a general listing of items to pack for your knitting journey.

Yarn: Yarns for the projects in this book were chosen from a variety of sources with the understanding that we all have personal preferences, budgets, and tastes. Detailed information about the yarns used to make the samples is provided. Patterns also include yarn weight symbols (see page 138) to assist you in choosing equivalent yarns. Knitting is about freedom--to use what you like to make what you want. As long as you obtain the proper gauge with a yarn of similar fiber content, you may substitute some of your favorite yarns. Generally, textured stitch patterns look their best in smooth, classic yarns, in colors neither too light nor too dark.

Your exquisite stitch work may get lost in busy novelty or multicolored yarns.

Straight Knitting needles: Are available in 10" (25.5 cm) and 14" (35.5 cm) lengths, use the length that works best for your project.

Circular Knitting needles: For the blanket and throw patterns on pages 66 and 68, you will need long circular needles to accommodate the number of stitches. For necklines and armholes on some of the garments, 16" (40.5 cm) circular needles are used.

Gauge ruler and tape measure: Used to measure gauge swatches and the length of knitted pieces.

Scissors: To snip off yarn ends.

Yarn needle: Used for weaving in ends and seaming. Use a needle with an eye of sufficient size for the yarn used.

Stitch holders: Used to hold live stitches for later use. Most garment patterns have the back neck stitches put onto a stitch holder rather than binding them off and picking them up again.

Stitch markers: You may find stitch markers helpful and some patterns advise as to their placement, but once you've completed a few rows, it will be easy to see what comes next without them.

Row counter: As with stitch markers, you may find a row counter helpful for keeping your place on some of the longer stitch patterns.

Crochet hook: Used for picking up dropped stitches and correcting mistakes. Use a hook in a size similar to that of the knitting needles. It can also be helpful to use when picking up stitches.

UNDERSTANDING STITCH MULTIPLES AND CHARTS

Each stitch in the Stitch Gallery includes a stitch multiple and a chart.
If you're unfamiliar with the information, please review this section before you begin!

STITCH MULTIPLE BASICS

Below is an example of a stitch pattern as you would find it in the Stitch Gallery.

EXAMPLE
SMALL BASKET {10 +5 x 8}

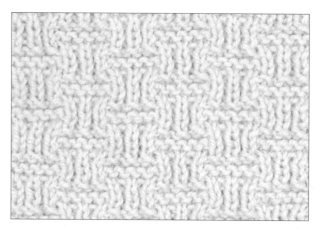

Stitch Multiple—The numbers enclosed in brackets { } are the stitch multiple which indicates the number of stitches and rows the pattern must be worked. The numbers for Small Basket pattern are: {10 + 5 x 8}. The first number in the set {10} is the stitch multiple, which can be multiplied by any number to reach the number of stitches needed for the width required: 10, 20, 30, 40, 50, etc. To that number, we must add the second number {5} which is required in flat (back and forth) knitting to balance the pattern across the row. We now have the number to cast on when using this stitch: (Multiple of) 10 + 5 = 15, 25, 35, 45, 55, etc. The third number in the set is the number of rows required to complete the pattern. Depending on the desired length of the piece, this pattern could be worked for 8, 16, 24, 32, 40 (and so on) rows.

Row 1 (Right side)**:** [(K1, P1) twice, K6] across to last 5 sts, K1, (P1, K1) twice.

Row 2: P1, (K1, P1) twice, [K5, P1, (K1, P1) twice] across.

Rows 3 and 4: Repeat Rows 1 and 2.

Row 5: [K6, (P1, K1) twice] across to last 5 sts, K5.

Row 6: K5, [P1, (K1, P1) twice, K5] across.

Rows 7 and 8: Repeat Rows 5 and 6.

Repeat Rows 1-8 for pattern.

READING A CHART

A knitting chart is simply a visual representation of the right, or front side, of the work. Charts are worked from bottom to top. Odd-numbered rows are read from right to left, just as stitches are worked right to left across the needle. Even-numbered rows are read from left to right. Repeats are indicated by brackets beneath the chart.

Often, the chart includes more than one repeat, allowing you to see the full pattern.

On right-side (odd-numbered) rows, the white square indicates a knit stitch, and the shaded square a purl.

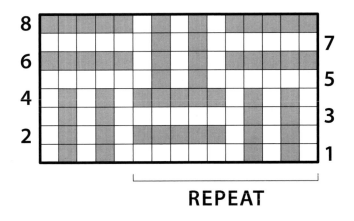

REPEAT

Key
☐ - knit on **right** side rows; purl on **wrong** side rows
▨ - purl on **right** side rows; knit on **wrong** side rows

TIP

If you're a new knitter, it's helpful to be able to identify knit and purl stitches.

The knit stitch is a smooth, V-shaped stitch.

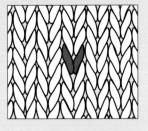

The purl stitch is a rounded little bump or nub.

With practice, you will find yourself "reading" the knitting rather than instructions or charts.

STITCH GALLERY

1. GARTER STITCH

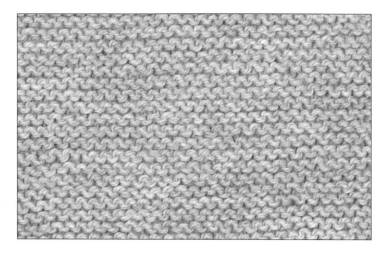

{Any x Any}

Knit every row.

2. SEED

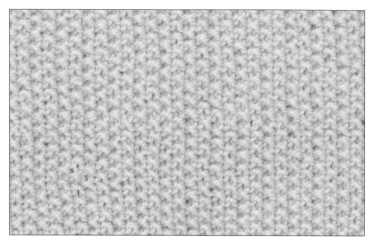

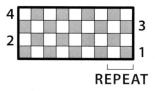

REPEAT

{2 + 1 x 1}

Row 1 (Right side)**:** [P1, K1] across to last st, P1.

Repeat Row 1 for pattern.

3. 1 x 1 RIB

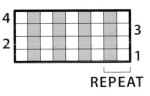

REPEAT

{2 + 1 x 2}

Row 1 (Right side)**:** [K1, P1] across to last st, K1.

Row 2: P1, [K1, P1] across.

Repeat Rows 1 and 2 for pattern.

4. BROKEN RIB

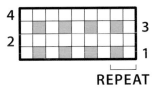

REPEAT

{2 + 1 x 2}

Row 1 (Right side)**:** [K1, P1] across to last st, K1.

Row 2: Purl across.

Repeat Rows 1 and 2 for pattern.

5. SAND

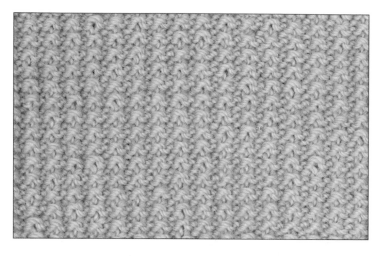

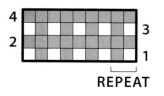

REPEAT

{2 + 1 x 2}

Row 1 (Right side)**:** [K1, P1] across to last st, K1.

Row 2: Knit across.

Repeat Rows 1 and 2 for pattern.

6. KNITS AND PURLS

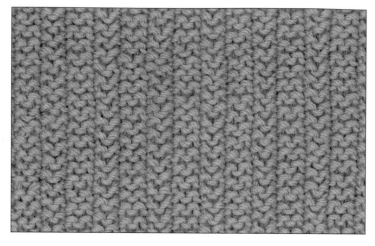

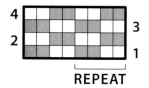

REPEAT

{4 x 2}

Row 1 (Right side)**:** [K2, P2] across.

Row 2: [P2, K2] across.

Repeat Rows 1 and 2 for pattern.

7. 2 x 2 RIB

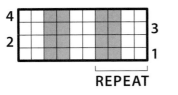

REPEAT

{4 + 2 x 2}

Row 1 (Right side)**:** [K2, P2] across to last 2 sts, K2.

Row 2: P2, [K2, P2] across.

Repeat Rows 1 and 2 for pattern.

8. MISTAKE RIB

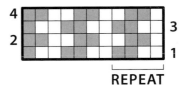

REPEAT

{4 + 3 x 2}

Row 1: [K2, P2] across to last 3 sts, K2, P1.

Row 2: K2, P1, [P1, K2, P1] across.

Repeat Rows 1 and 2 for pattern.

9. BEADED RIB

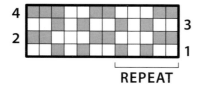

{5 + 2 x 2}

Row 1 (Right side): **[K2, P1, K1, P1]** across to last 2 sts, K2.

Row 2: K2, [P3, K2] across.

Repeat Rows 1 and 2 for pattern.

10. CARTRIDGE RIB

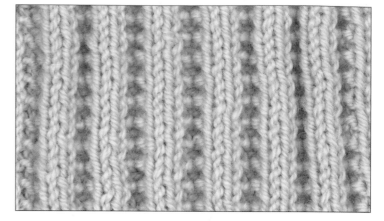

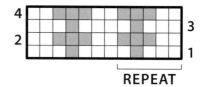

{5 + 2 x 2}

Row 1 (Right side): **[K3, P1, K1]** across to last 2 sts, K2.

Row 2: P2, [K3, P2] across.

Repeat Rows 1 and 2 for pattern.

11. TWIN RIB

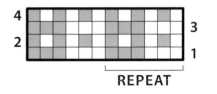

REPEAT

{6 x 2}

Row 1 (Right side): [K3, P3] across.

Row 2: [K1, P1] across.

Repeat Rows 1 and 2 for pattern.

12. MODIFIED SEED

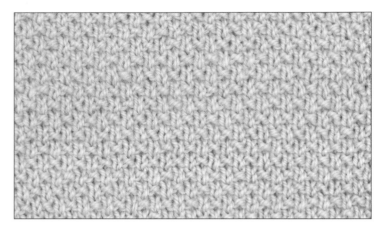

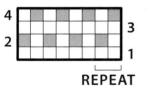

REPEAT

{2 x 4}

Row 1 (Right side): Knit across.

Row 2: [K1, P1] across.

Row 3: Knit across.

Row 4: [P1, K1] across.

Repeat Rows 1-4 for pattern.

13. MOSS

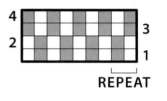

{2 + 1 x 4}

Row 1 (Right side): [K1, P1] across to last st, K1.

Row 2: P1, [K1, P1] across.

Row 3: [P1, K1] across to last st, P1.

Row 4: K1, [P1, K1] across.

Repeat Rows 1-4 for pattern.

14. WAFFLE STITCH

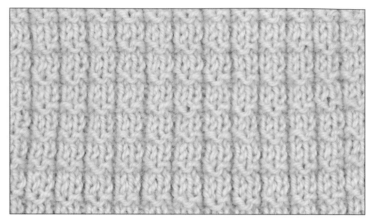

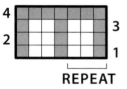

{3 + 1 x 4}

Row 1 (Right side): [P1, K2] across to last st, P1.

Row 2: K1, [P2, K1] across.

Row 3: [P1, K2] across to last st, P1.

Row 4: Knit across.

Repeat Rows 1-4 for pattern.

15. 3 AND 1

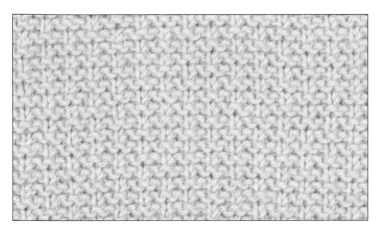

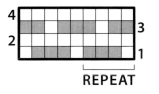

REPEAT

{4 + 1 x 4}

Row 1 (Right side)**:** [K1, P3] across to last st, K1.

Row 2: Purl across.

Row 3: [P2, K1, P1] across to last st, P1.

Row 4: Purl across.

Repeat Rows 1-4 for pattern.

16. SIMPLE TEXTURE

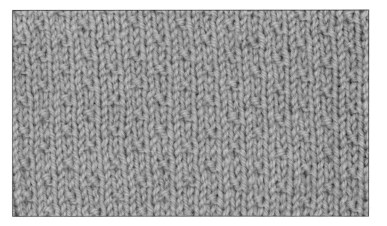

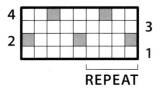

REPEAT

{4 + 1 x 4}

Row 1 (Right side)**:** Knit across.

Row 2: K1, [P3, K1] across.

Row 3: Knit across.

Row 4: P1, [P1, K1, P2] across.

Repeat Rows 1-4 for pattern.

17. DOUBLE MOSS

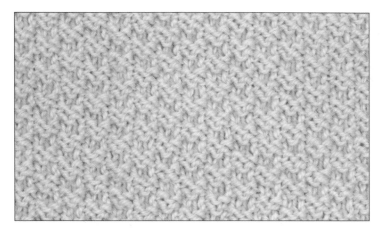

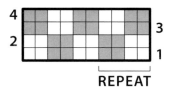

REPEAT

{4 + 2 x 4}

Row 1 (Right side): [K2, P2] across to last 2 sts, K2.

Row 2: P2, [K2, P2] across.

Row 3: [P2, K2] across to last 2 sts, P2.

Row 4: K2, [P2, K2] across.

Repeat Rows 1-4 for pattern.

18. DOUBLE MOSS RIB

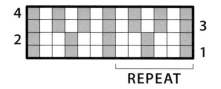

REPEAT

{6 + 1 x 4}

Row 1 (Right side): [P1, K2] across to last st, P1.

Row 2: K1, [P2, K1] across.

Row 3: [P1, K1] across to last st, P1.

Row 4: K1, [P1, K1] across.

Repeat Rows 1-4 for pattern.

19. DOUBLE FLECK

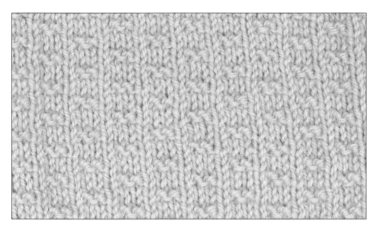

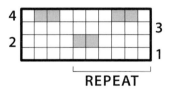

REPEAT

{6 + 4 x 4}

Row 1 (Right side): Knit across.

Row 2: P4, [K2, P4] across.

Row 3: Knit across.

Row 4: P1, K2, P1, [P3, K2, P1] across.

Repeat Rows 1-4 for pattern.

20. TRIANGLE RIB

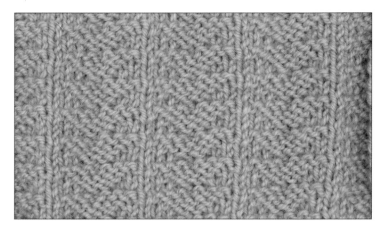

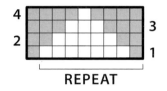

REPEAT

{8 + 1 x 4}

Row 1 (Right side): [P1, K7] across to last st, P1.

Row 2: K1, [K1, P5, K2] across.

Row 3: [P3, K3, P2] across to last st, P1.

Row 4: K1, [K3, P1, K4] across.

Repeat Rows 1-4 for pattern.

21. LITTLE ARROWS

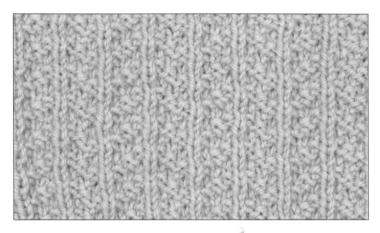

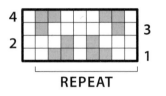

REPEAT

{8 + 1 x 4}

Row 1 (Right side)**:** [K2, (P2, K1) twice] across to last st, K1.

Row 2: P1, [P2, K1, P1, K1, P3] across.

Row 3: [K1, P1, K5, P1] across to last st, K1.

Row 4: P1, [K2, P3, K2, P1] across.

Repeat Rows 1-4 for pattern.

22. OPEN CHEVRON

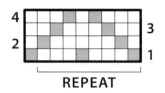

REPEAT

{8 + 1 x 4}

Row 1 (Right side)**:** [P1, K3] across to last st, P1.

Row 2: P1, [K1, P5, K1, P1] across.

Row 3: [K2, P1, K3, P1, K1] across to last st, K1.

Row 4: P1, [P2, K1, P1, K1, P3] across.

Repeat Rows 1-4 for pattern.

23. ZIGZAG RIB

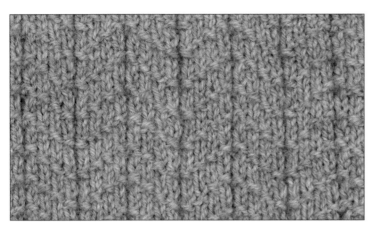

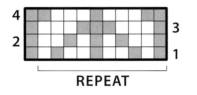

{10 + 1 x 4}

Row 1 (Right side)**:** [P1, K1, (P1, K2) twice, P1, K1] across to last st, P1.

Row 2: K1, [P2, K1, (P1, K1) twice, P2, K1] across.

Row 3: [P1, K3, P3, K3] across to last st, P1.

Row 4: K1, [(K1, P3) twice, K2] across.

Repeat Rows 1-4 for pattern.

24. WAVE

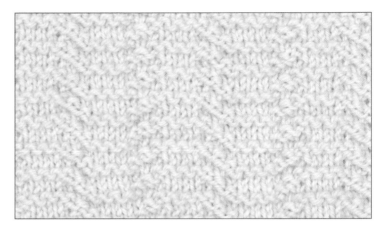

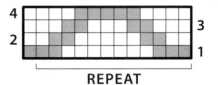

{12 + 1 x 4}

Row 1 (Right side)**:** [P3, K7, P2] across to last st, P1.

Row 2: P1, [P1, K2, P5, K2, P2] across.

Row 3: [K3, P2) twice, K2] across to last st, K1.

Row 4: P1, [P3, K5, P4] across.

Repeat Rows 1-4 for pattern.

25. SINGLE BASKET WEAVE

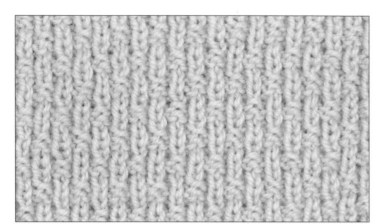

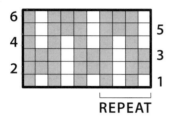

REPEAT

{4 + 2 x 6}

Row 1 (Right side)**:** [K1, P1] across.

Row 2: K2, [K1, P1, K2] across.

Row 3: [P2, K1, P1] across to last 2 sts, P2.

Row 4: [K1, P1] across.

Row 5: [K1, P3] across to last 2 sts, K1, P1.

Row 6: K1, P1, [K3, P1] across.

Repeat Rows 1-6 for pattern.

26. LATTICE

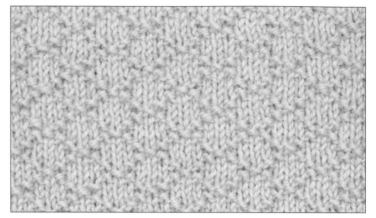

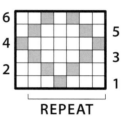

REPEAT

{6 + 1 x 6}

Row 1 (Right side)**:** [K3, P1, K2] across to last st, K1.

Row 2: P1, [(P1, K1) twice, P2] across.

Row 3: [K1, P1, K3, P1] across to last st, K1.

Row 4: K1, [P5, K1] across.

Row 5: [K1, P1, K3, P1] across to last st, K1.

Row 6: P1, [(P1, K1) twice, P2] across.

Repeat Rows 1-6 for pattern.

27. LITTLE PYRAMID

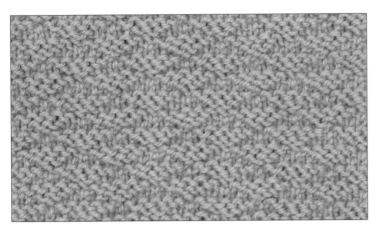

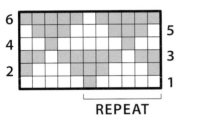

{6 + 5 x 6}

Row 1 (Right side)**:** [K5, P1] across to last 5 sts, K5.

Row 2: K1, P3, K1, [K2, P3, K1] across.

Row 3: [P2, K1, P3] across to last 5 sts, P2, K1, P2.

Row 4: P2, K1, P2, [P3, K1, P2] across.

Row 5: [K1, P3, K2] across to last 5 sts, K1, P3, K1.

Row 6: K5, [P1, K5] across.

Repeat Rows 1-6 for pattern.

28. REVERSE STOCKING CHREVRONS

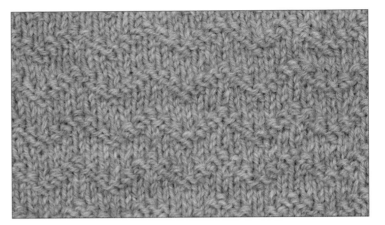

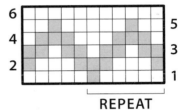

{6 + 5 x 6}

Row 1 (Right side)**:** [K5, P1] across to last 5 sts, K5.

Row 2: K1, P3, K1, [K2, P3, K1] across.

Row 3: [P2, K1] across to last 2 sts, P2.

Row 4: P1, K3, P1, [P2, K3, P1] across.

Row 5: [K2, P1, K3] across to last 5 sts, K2, P1, K2.

Row 6: Purl across.

Repeat Rows 1-6 for pattern.

29. LADDER

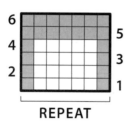

REPEAT

{7 x 6}

Row 1 (Right side)**:** [P1, K5, P1] across.

Row 2: [K1, P5, K1] across.

Rows 3 and 4: Repeat Rows 1 and 2.

Row 5: Purl across.

Row 6: Knit across.

Repeat Rows 1-6 for pattern.

30. RIPPLE STRIPE

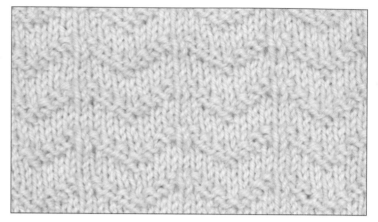

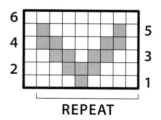

REPEAT

{8 + 1 x 6}

Row 1 (Right side)**:** [K4, P1, K3] across to last st, K1.

Row 2: P1, [P2, K3, P3] across.

Row 3: [K2, (P2, K1) twice] across to last st, K1.

Row 4: P1, [K2, P3, K2, P1] across.

Row 5: [K1, P1, K5, P1] across to last st, K1.

Row 6: Purl across.

Repeat Rows 1-6 for pattern.

31. MOSS RIB

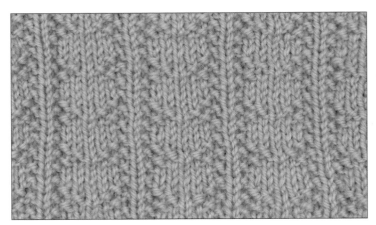

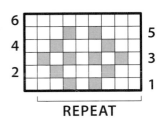

REPEAT

{8 + 1 x 6}

Row 1 (Right side)**:** [K3, P1, K1, P1, K2] across to last st, K1.

Row 2: P1, [P1, K1, P3, K1, P2] across.

Row 3: [K1, P1] across to last st, K1.

Row 4: P1, [P1, K1, P3, K1, P2] across.

Row 5: [K3, P1, K1, P1, K2] across to last st, K1.

Row 6: Purl across.

Repeat Rows 1-6 for pattern.

32. BASKET WEAVE

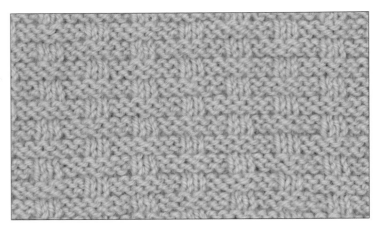

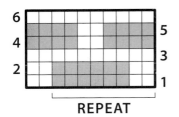

REPEAT

{8 + 2 x 6}

Row 1 (Right side)**:** [K2, P6] across to last 2 sts, K2.

Row 2: P2, [K6, P2] across.

Row 3: Knit across.

Row 4: K2, [K2, P2, K4] across.

Row 5: [P4, K2, P2] across to last 2 sts, P2.

Row 6: Purl across.

Repeat Rows 1-6 for pattern.

33. DIAGONAL RIB

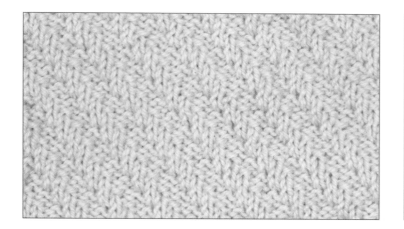

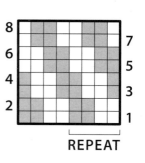

REPEAT

{4 x 8}

Row 1 (Right side): [K2, P2] across.

Row 2: [K2, P2] across.

Row 3: [P1, K2, P1] across.

Row 4: [K1, P2, K1] across.

Rows 5 and 6: [P2, K2] across.

Row 7: [K1, P2, K1] across.

Row 8: [P1, K2, P1) across.

Repeat Rows 1-8 for pattern.

34. EMBOSSED

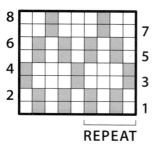

REPEAT

{4 + 1 x 8}

Row 1 (Right side): [K1, P1] across to last st, K1.

Row 2: P1, [K1, P1] across.

Row 3: [P1, K3] across to last st, P1.

Row 4: K1, [P3, K1] across.

Row 5: [K1, P1] across to last st, K1.

Row 6: P1, [K1, P1] across.

Row 7: [K2, P1, K1] across to last st, K1.

Row 8: P1, [P1, K1, P2] across.

Repeat Rows 1-8 for pattern.

35. BABY WEAVE

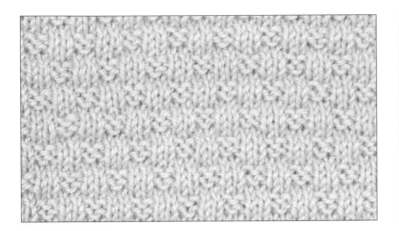

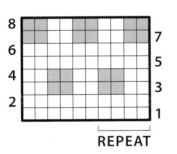

REPEAT

{4 + 2 x 8}

Row 1 (Right side)**:** Knit across.

Row 2: Purl across.

Row 3: [K2, P2] across to last 2 sts, K2.

Row 4: P2, [K2, P2] across.

Row 5: Knit across.

Row 6: Purl across.

Row 7: [P2, K2] across to last 2 sts, P2.

Row 8: K2, [P2, K2] across.

Repeat Rows 1-8 for pattern.

36. VERTICAL PARALLELOGRAMS

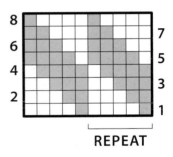

REPEAT

{5 x 8}

Row 1 (Right side)**:** [P1, K4] across.

Rows 2 and 3: [P3, K2] across.

Row 4: [P1, K4] across.

Row 5: [K1, P4] across.

Rows 6 and 7: [K3, P2] across.

Row 8: [K1, P4] across.

Repeat Rows 1-8 for pattern.

37. SWEDISH BLOCK

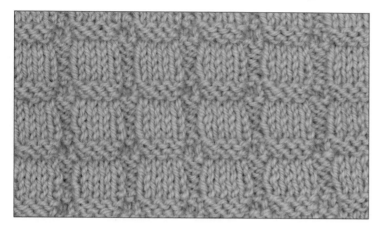

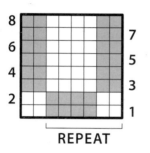

REPEAT

{6 + 2 x 8}

Row 1 (Right side): [K2, P4] across to last 2 sts, K2.

Row 2: P2, [K4, P2] across.

Row 3: [P2, K4] across to last 2 sts, P2.

Row 4: K2, [P4, K2] across.

Rows 5-8: Repeat Rows 3 and 4 twice.

Repeat Rows 1-8 for pattern.

38. SMALL CHECKS

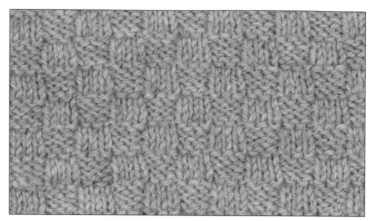

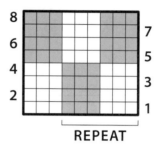

REPEAT

{6 + 3 x 8}

Row 1 (Right side): [K3, P3] across to last 3 sts, K3.

Row 2: P3, [K3, P3] across.

Rows 3 and 4: Repeat Rows 1 and 2.

Row 5: [P3, K3] across to last 3 sts, P3.

Row 6: K3, [P3, K3] across.

Rows 7 and 8: Repeat Rows 5 and 6.

Repeat Rows 1-8 for pattern.

39. LITTLE KNOT

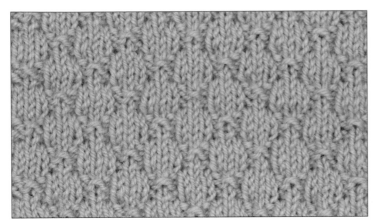

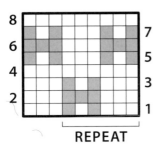

REPEAT

{6 + 3 x 8}

Row 1 (Right side): **[**K3, P1, K1, P1**]** across to last 3 sts, K3.

Row 2: P3, **[**K3, P3**]** across.

Row 3: **[**K3, P1, K1, P1**]** across to last 3 sts, K3.

Row 4: Purl across.

Row 5: **[**P1, K1, P1, K3**]** across to last 3 sts, P1, K1, P1.

Row 6: K3, **[**P3, K3**]** across.

Row 7: **[**P1, K1, P1, K3**]** across to last 3 sts, P1, K1, P1.

Row 8: Purl across.

Repeat Rows 1-8 for pattern.

40. SUGAR CUBES

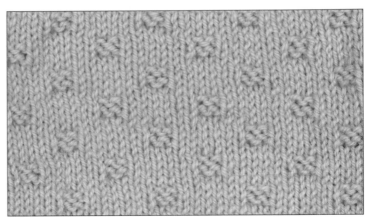

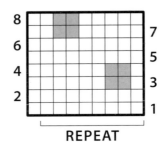

REPEAT

{8 + 1 x 8}

Row 1 (Right side): Knit across.

Row 2: Purl across.

Row 3: **[**K1, P2, K5**]** across to last st, K1.

Row 4: P1, **[**P5, K2, P1**]** across.

Rows 5 and 6: Repeat Rows 1 and 2.

Row 7: **[**K5, P2, K1**]** across to last st, K1.

Row 8: P1, **[**P1, K2, P5**]** across.

Repeat Rows 1-8 for pattern.

41. DIAMOND PANELS

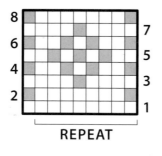

REPEAT

{8 + 1 x 8}

Row 1 (Right side)**:** Knit across.

Row 2: K1, [P7, K1] across.

Row 3: [K4, P1, K3] across to last st, K1.

Row 4: K1, [P2, K1, P1, K1, P2, K1] across.

Row 5: [K2, (P1, K1) 3 times] across to last st, K1.

Row 6: K1, [P2, K1, P1, K1, P2, K1] across.

Row 7: [K4, P1, K3] across to last st, K1.

Row 8: K1, [P7, K1] across.

Repeat Rows 1-8 for pattern.

42. DIAMOND BROCADE

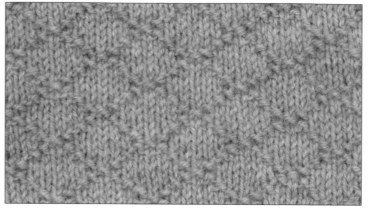

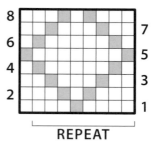

REPEAT

{8 + 1 x 8}

Row 1 (Right side)**:** [K4, P1, K3] across to last st, K1.

Row 2: P1, [P2, K1, P1, K1, P3] across.

Row 3: [K2, P1, K3, P1, K1] across to last st, K1.

Row 4: P1, [K1, P5, K1, P1] across.

Row 5: [P1, K7] across to last st, P1.

Row 6: P1, [K1, P5, K1, P1] across.

Row 7: [K2, P1, K3, P1, K1] across to last st, K1.

Row 8: P1, [P2, K1, P1, K1, P3] across.

Repeat Rows 1-8 for pattern.

43. TEXTURED RIB

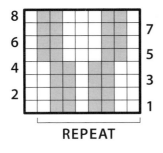

REPEAT

{8 + 1 x 8}

Row 1 (Right side)**:** [K2, (P2, K1) twice] across to last st, K1.

Row 2: P1, [(P1, K2) twice, P2] across.

Rows 3 and 4: Repeat Rows 1 and 2.

Row 5: [K1, P2, K3, P2] across to last st, K1.

Row 6: P1, [K2, P3, K2, P1] across.

Rows 7 and 8: Repeat Rows 5 and 6.

Repeat Rows 1-8 for pattern.

44. DIAMONDS AND PURLS

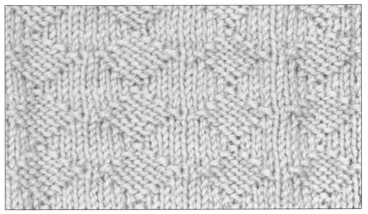

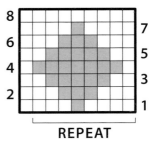

REPEAT

{8 + 1 x 8}

Row 1 (Right side)**:** [K4, P1, K3] across to last st, K1.

Row 2: P1, [P2, K3, P3] across.

Row 3: [K2, P5, K1] across to last st, K1.

Row 4: P1, [K7, P1] across.

Row 5: [K2, P5, K1] across to last st, K1.

Row 6: P1, [P2, K3, P3] across.

Row 7: [K4, P1, K3] across to last st, K1.

Row 8: Purl across.

Repeat Rows 1-8 for pattern.

45. DIAGONALS

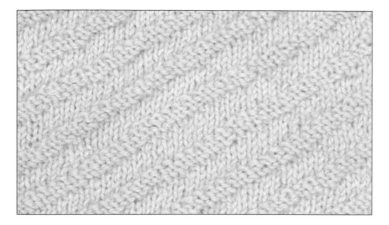

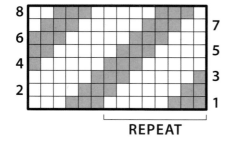

REPEAT

{8 + 6 x 8}

Row 1 (Right side)**:** [P3, K5] across to last 6 sts, P3, K3.

Row 2: P4, K2, [K1, P5, K2] across.

Row 3: [P1, K5, P2] across to last 6 sts, P1, K5.

Row 4: K1, P5, [K3, P5] across.

Row 5: [K4, P3, K1] across to last 6 sts, K4, P2.

Row 6: K3, P3, [P2, K3, P3] across.

Row 7: [K2, P3, K3] across to last 6 sts, K2, P3, K1.

Row 8: P2, K3, P1, [P4, K3, P1] across.

Repeat Rows 1-8 for pattern.

46. SMALL BASKET

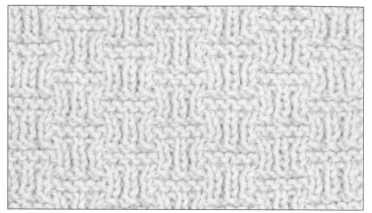

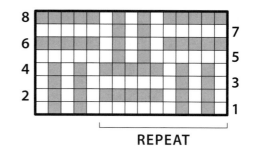

REPEAT

{10 + 5 x 8}

Row 1 (Right side)**:** [(K1, P1) twice, K6] across to last 5 sts, K1, (P1, K1) twice.

Row 2: P1, (K1, P1) twice, [K5, P1, (K1, P1) twice] across.

Rows 3 and 4: Repeat Rows 1 and 2.

Row 5: [K6, (P1, K1) twice] across to last 5 sts, K5.

Row 6: K5, [P1, (K1, P1) twice, K5] across.

Rows 7 and 8: Repeat Rows 5 and 6.

Repeat Rows 1-8 for pattern.

47. FANCY TRACK

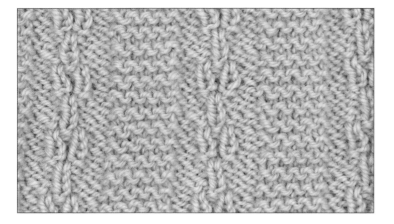

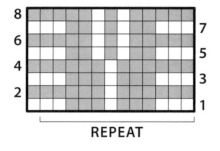

REPEAT

{12 + 1 x 8}

Row 1 (Right side): [K3, P3, K1, P3, K2] across to last st, K1.

Row 2: K1, [K5, P1, K6] across.

Rows 3 and 4: Repeat Rows 1 and 2.

Row 5: [K3, P2, K1, P1, K1, P2, K2] across to last st, K1.

Row 6: K1, [K4, P1, K1, P1, K5] across.

Rows 7 and 8: Repeat Rows 5 and 6.

Repeat Rows 1-8 for pattern.

48. MOSS ZIGZAG

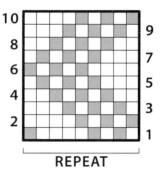

REPEAT

{9 x 10}

Row 1 (Right side): [(K1, P1) twice, K4, P1] across.

Row 2: [P4, K1, (P1, K1) twice] across.

Row 3: [(K1, P1) 3 times, K3] across.

Row 4: [P2, K1, (P1, K1) twice, P2] across.

Row 5: [K3, (P1, K1) 3 times] across.

Row 6: [K1, (P1, K1) twice, P4] across.

Row 7: [K3, (P1, K1) 3 times] across.

Row 8: [P2, K1, (P1, K1) twice, P2] across.

Row 9: [(K1, P1) 3 times, K3] across.

Row 10: [P4, K1, (P1, K1) twice] across.

Repeat Rows 1-10 for pattern.

49. WOVEN SQUARES

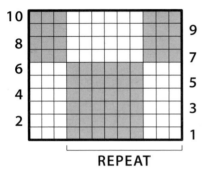

REPEAT

{9 + 3 x 10}

Row 1 (Right side)**:** [K3, P6] across to last 3 sts, K3.

Row 2: P3, [K6, P3] across.

Rows 3-6: Repeat Rows 1 and 2 twice.

Row 7: [P3, K6] across to last 3 sts, P3.

Row 8: K3, [P6, K3] across.

Rows 9 and 10: Repeat Rows 7 and 8.

Repeat Rows 1-10 for pattern.

50. PETITE SEED DIAMONDS

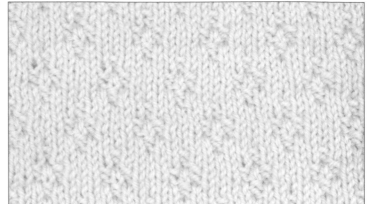

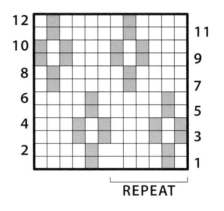

REPEAT

{6 x 12}

Row 1 (Right side)**:** [K1, P1, K4] across.

Row 2: [P4, K1, P1] across.

Row 3: [P1, K1, P1, K3] across.

Row 4: [P3, K1, P1, K1] across.

Rows 5 and 6: Repeat Rows 1 and 2.

Row 7: [K4, P1, K1] across.

Row 8: [P1, K1, P4] across.

Row 9: [K3, P1, K1, P1] across.

Row 10: [K1, P1, K1, P3] across.

Rows 11 and 12: Repeat Rows 7 and 8.

Repeat Rows 1-12 for pattern.

51. KNIT AND RIB

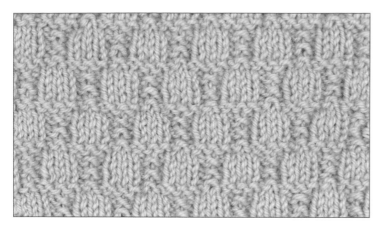

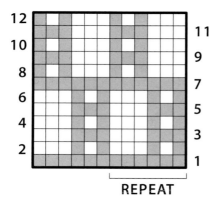

REPEAT

{6 x 12}

Row 1 (Right side)**:** Purl across.

Row 2: [P3, K1, P1, K1] across.

Row 3: [P3, K3] across.

Rows 4-6: Repeat Rows 2 and 3 once, then repeat Row 2 once **more**.

Row 7: Purl across.

Row 8: [K1, P1, K1, P3] across.

Row 9: [K3, P3] across.

Rows 10-12: Repeat Rows 8 and 9 once, then repeat Row 8 once **more**.

Repeat Rows 1-12 for pattern.

52. GARTER ZIGZAG

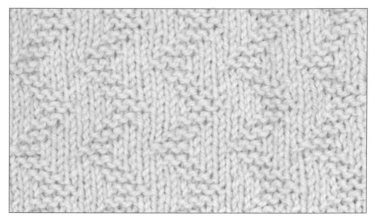

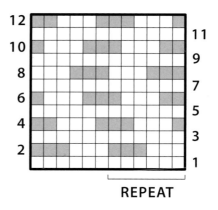

REPEAT

{6 x 12}

Row 1 AND ALL RIGHT SIDE ROWS (Right side)**:** Knit across.

Row 2: [K3, P3] across.

Row 4: [K2, P3, K1] across.

Row 6: [K1, P3, K2] across.

Row 8: [P3, K3] across.

Row 10: [K1, P3, K2] across.

Row 12: [K2, P3, K1] across.

Repeat Rows 1-12 for pattern.

53. WAVY RIB

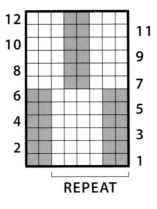

REPEAT

{6 + 2 x 12}

Row 1 (Right side)**:** [P2, K4] across to last 2 sts, P2.

Row 2: K2, [P4, K2] across.

Rows 3-6: Repeat Rows 1 and 2 twice.

Row 7: [K3, P2, K1] across to last 2 sts, K2.

Row 8: P2, [P1, K2, P3] across.

Rows 9-12: Repeat Rows 7 and 8 twice.

Repeat Rows 1-12 for pattern.

54. MIRRORED TRIANGLE

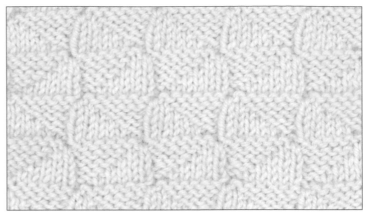

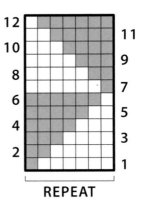

REPEAT

{7 x 12}

Row 1 (Right side)**:** [K6, P1] across.

Row 2: [K2, P5] across.

Rows 3 and 4: [K4, P3] across.

Row 5: [K2, P5] across.

Row 6: [K6, P1] across.

Row 7: [P1, K6] across.

Row 8: [P5, K2] across.

Rows 9 and 10: [P3, K4] across.

Row 11: [P5, K2] across.

Row 12: [P1, K6] across.

Repeat Rows 1-12 for pattern.

55. BASKET WEAVE RIB

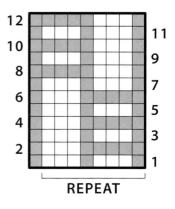

REPEAT

{8 + 1 x 12}

Row 1 (Right side): [P1, K3] across to last st, P1.

Row 2: K1, [P3, K5] across.

Rows 3-6: Repeat Rows 1 and 2 twice.

Row 7: [P1, K3] across to last st, P1.

Row 8: K1, [K4, P3, K1] across.

Rows 9-12: Repeat Rows 7 and 8 twice.

Repeat Rows 1-12 for pattern.

56. GARTER STITCH COLUMNS

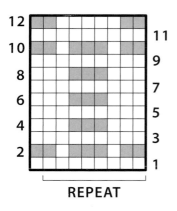

REPEAT

{8 + 1 x 12}

Row 1 (Right side): Knit across.

Row 2: K1, [K1, P1, K3, P1, K2] across.

Row 3: Knit across.

Row 4: P1, [P2, K3, P3] across.

Rows 5-8: Repeat Rows 3 and 4 twice.

Rows 9-11: Repeat Rows 1 and 2 once, then repeat Row 1 once **more**.

Row 12: K1, [K1, P5, K2] across.

Repeat Rows 1-12 for pattern.

57. LOZENGE

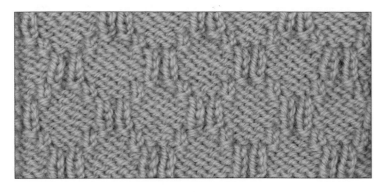

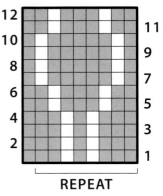

REPEAT

{8 + 1 x 12}

Row 1 (Right side)**:** [P3, K1, P1, K1, P2] across to last st, P1.

Row 2: K1, [K2, P1, K1, P1, K3] across.

Rows 3 and 4: Repeat Rows 1 and 2.

Row 5: [P2, K1, P3, K1, P1] across to last st, P1.

Row 6: K1, [K1, P1, K3, P1, K2] across.

Row 7: [P1, K1, P5, K1] across to last st, P1.

Row 8: K1, [P1, K5, P1, K1] across.

Rows 9 and 10: Repeat Rows 7 and 8.

Rows 11 and 12: Repeat Rows 5 and 6.

Repeat Rows 1-12 for pattern.

58. MOSS DIAMONDS

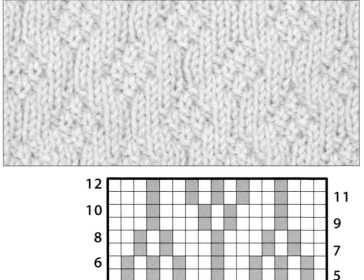

REPEAT

{10 + 7 x 12}

Row 1 (Right side)**:** [(K3, P1) twice, K1, P1] across to last 7 sts, K3, P1, K3.

Row 2: P3, K1, P3, [K1, P1, (K1, P3) twice] across.

Row 3: [K2, P1, K1, P1, K3, P1, K1] across to last 7 sts, K2, P1, K1, P1, K2.

Row 4: P2, K1, P1, K1, P2, [P1, K1, P3, K1, P1, K1, P2] across.

Row 5: [(K1, P1) 3 times, K2, P1, K1] across to last 7 sts, K1, (P1, K1) 3 times.

Row 6: P1, (K1, P1) 3 times, [P1, K1, P2, (K1, P1) 3 times] across.

Rows 7 and 8: Repeat Rows 3 and 4.

Rows 9 and 10: Repeat Rows 1 and 2.

Row 11: ★ K3, P1, K2, (P1, K1) twice; repeat from ★ across to last 7 sts, P1, K2, P1, K3.

Row 12: P3, K1, P2, K1, ★ (P1, K1) twice, P2, K1, P3; repeat from ★ across.

Repeat Rows 1-12 for pattern.

59. SCALES

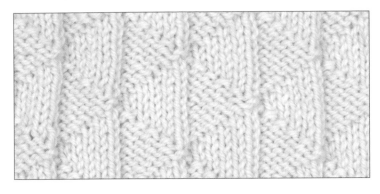

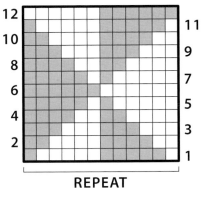

REPEAT

{12 x 12}

Row 1 (Right side)**:** [K1, P5, K5, P1] across.

Row 2: [K2, P4, K4, P2] across.

Row 3: [K3, P3] across.

Row 4: [K4, P2, K2, P4] across.

Row 5: [K5, P1, K1, P5] across.

Row 6: [K6, P6] across.

Row 7: [K5, P1, K1, P5] across.

Row 8: [K4, P2, K2, P4] across.

Row 9: [K3, P3] across.

Row 10: [K2, P4, K4, P2] across.

Row 11: [K1, P5, K5, P1] across.

Row 12: [P6, K6] across.

Repeat Rows 1-12 for pattern.

60. KING CHARLES

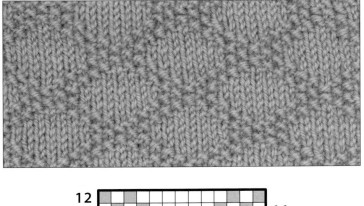

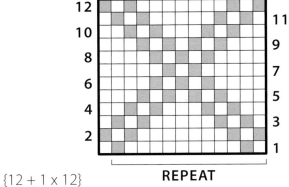

{12 + 1 x 12}

REPEAT

Row 1 (Right side)**:** [K1, P1, K9, P1] across to last st, K1.

Row 2: K1, [P1, K1, P7, K1, P1, K1] across.

Row 3: [(K1, P1) twice, K5, P1, K1, P1] across to last st, K1.

Row 4: P1, [(P1, K1) twice, P3, K1, P1, K1, P2] across.

Row 5: [K3, P1, (K1, P1) 3 times, K2] across to last st, K1.

Row 6: P1, [P3, K1, (P1, K1) twice, P4] across.

Row 7: [K5, P1, K1, P1, K4] across to last st, K1.

Row 8: P1, [P3, K1, (P1, K1) twice, P4] across.

Row 9: [K3, P1, (K1, P1) 3 times, K2] across to last st, K1.

Row 10: P1, [(P1, K1) twice, P3, K1, P1, K1, P2] across.

Row 11: [(K1, P1) twice, K5, P1, K1, P1] across to last st, K1.

Row 12: K1, [P1, K1, P7, K1, P1, K1] across.

Repeat Rows 1-12 for pattern.

61. MOSS AND RIB BLOCKS

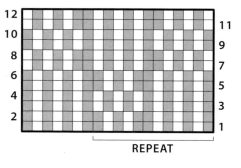

{12 + 7 x 12}

Row 1 (Right side): [(P1, K1) 3 times, P2, (K1, P1) twice] across to last 7 sts, P1, (K1, P1) 3 times.

Row 2: K1, (P1, K1) 3 times, [(K1, P1) twice, K2, (P1, K1) 3 times] across.

Row 3: [P1, K1) across to last st, P1.

Row 4: K1, [P1, K1) across.

Rows 5 and 6: Repeat Rows 1 and 2.

Row 7: [K1, (P1, K1) twice, P2, K1, (P1, K1) twice] across to last 7 sts, P2, K1, (P1, K1) twice.

Row 8: P1, (K1, P1) twice, K2, [P1, (K1, P1) twice, K2, P1, (K1, P1) twice] across.

Rows 9 and 10: Repeat Rows 3 and 4.

Rows 11 and 12: Repeat Rows 7 and 8.

Repeat Rows 1-12 for pattern.

62. RIB AND DIAMOND

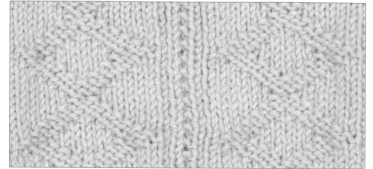

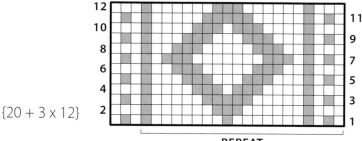

{20 + 3 x 12}

Row 1 (Right side):
[(K1, P1) twice, (K7, P1) twice] across to last 3 sts, K1, P1, K1.

Row 2: P3, [K1, P6, K3, P6, K1, P3] across.

Row 3: [(K1, P1) twice, K5, P5, K5, P1] across to last 3 sts, K1, P1, K1.

Row 4: P3, [K1, P4, K3, P1, K3, P4, K1, P3] across.

Row 5: [(K1, P1) twice, K3, (P3, K3) twice, P1] across to last 3 sts, K1, P1, K1.

Row 6: P3, [K1, P2, K3, P5, K3, P2, K1, P3] across.

Row 7: [K1, (P1, K1) twice, P3, K7, P3, K1, P1] across to last 3 sts, K1, P1, K1.

Row 8: P3, [K1, P2, K3, P5, K3, P2, K1, P3] across

Row 9: [(K1, P1) twice, K3, (P3, K3) twice, P1] across to last 3 sts, K1, P1, K1.

Row 10: P3, [K1, P4, K3, P1, K3, P4, K1, P3) across.

Row 11: [(K1, P1) twice, K5, P5, K5, P1] across to last 3 sts, K1, P1, K1.

Row 12: P3, [K1, P6, K3, P6, K1, P3) across.

Repeat Rows 1-12 for pattern.

63. GARTER CHECK

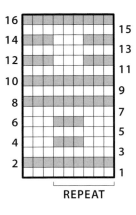

REPEAT

{6 + 3 x 16}

Rows 1-3: Knit across.

Row 4 (Wrong side)**:** P3, [K3, P3] across.

Rows 5 and 6: Repeat Rows 3 and 4.

Rows 7-11: Knit across.

Row 12: K3, [P3, K3] across.

Rows 13 and 14: Repeat Rows 11 and 12.

Rows 15 and 16: Knit across.

Repeat Rows 1-16 for pattern.

64. RIB AND WELT

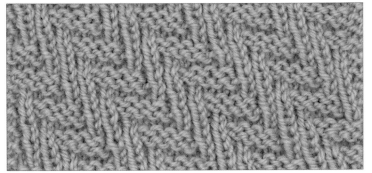

REPEAT

{8 x 16}

Row 1 (Right side)**:**
[K1, P1, K1, P5] across.

Row 2: [K5, P1, K1, P1] across.

Row 3: [K1, P1, K5, P1] across.

Rows 4 and 5: [K1, P5, K1, P1] across.

Row 6: [K1, P1, K5, P1] across.

Row 7: [K5, P1, K1, P1] across.

Row 8: [K1, P1, K1, P5] across.

Row 9: [P4, (K1, P1) twice] across.

Row 10: [(K1, P1) twice, K4] across.

Row 11: [K3, P1, K1, P1, K2] across.

Rows 12 and 13: [P2, K1, P1, K1, P3] across.

Row 14: [K3, P1, K1, P1, K2] across.

Row 15: [(K1, P1) twice, K4] across.

Row 16: [P4, (K1, P1) twice] across.

Repeat Rows 1-16 for pattern.

65. FLAME

{8 x 16}

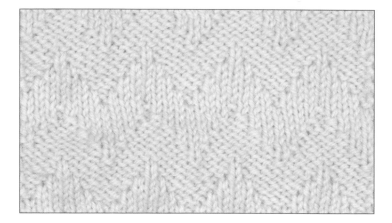

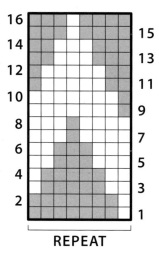

REPEAT

Row 1 (Right side):
[K1, P7] across.

Row 2: [K7, P1] across.

Row 3: [K2, P5, K1] across.

Row 4: [P1, K5, P2] across.

Row 5: [K3, P3, K2] across.

Row 6: [P2, K3, P3] across.

Row 7: [K4, P1, K3] across.

Row 8: [P3, K1, P4] across.

Row 9: [P1, K7] across.

Row 10: [P7, K1] across.

Row 11: [P2, K5, P1] across.

Row 12: [K1, P5, K2] across.

Row 13: [P3, K3, P2] across.

Row 14: [K2, P3, K3] across.

Row 15: [P4, K1, P3] across.

Row 16: [K3, P1, K4] across.

Repeat Rows 1-16 for pattern.

66. PINNACLE CHEVRON

{18 + 1 x 16}

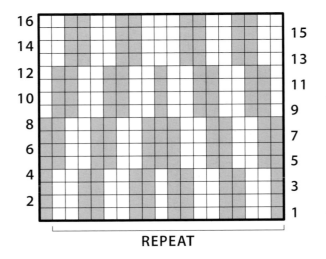

REPEAT

Row 1 (Right side): [P1, (K2, P2) twice, K1, (P2, K2) twice] across to last st, P1.

Row 2: K1, [(P2, K2) twice, P1, (K2, P2) twice, K1] across.

Rows 3 and 4: Repeat Rows 1 and 2.

Row 5: [(P2, K2) twice, P3, K2, P2, K2, P1] across to last st, P1.

Row 6: K1, [K1, P2, K2, P2, K3, (P2, K2) twice] across.

Rows 7 and 8: Repeat Rows 5 and 6.

Row 9: [K1, (P2, K2) twice, P1, (K2, P2) twice] across to last st, K1.

Row 10: P1, [(K2, P2) twice, K1, (P2, K2) twice, P1] across.

Rows 11 and 12: Repeat Rows 9 and 10.

Row 13: [(K2, P2) twice, K3, P2, K2, P2, K1] across to last st, K1.

Row 14: P1, [P1, K2, P2, K2, P3, (K2, P2) twice] across.

Rows 15 and 16: Repeat Rows 13 and 14.

Repeat Rows 1-16 for pattern.

67. DOUBLE BASKET

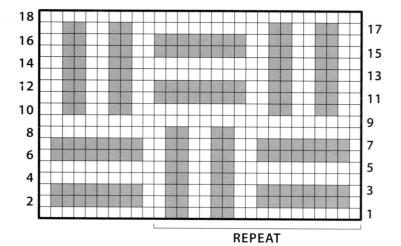

REPEAT

{18 + 10 x 18}

Row 1 (Right side)**:** [K 11, P2, K2, P2, K1) across to last 10 sts, K 10.

Row 2: P1, K8, P1, [P1, (K2, P2) twice, K8, P1] across.

Row 3: [K1, P8, (K2, P2) twice, K1] across to last 10 sts, K1, P8, K1.

Row 4: P 10, [P1, K2, P2, K2, P 11] across.

Rows 5-8: Repeat Rows 1-4.

Row 9: Knit across.

Row 10: P2, (K2, P2) twice, [P 10, (K2, P2) twice] across.

Row 11: [K2, (P2, K2) twice, P8] across to last 10 sts, K2, (P2, K2) twice.

Row 12: P2, (K2, P2) twice, [K8, P2, (K2, P2) twice] across.

Row 13: [(K2, P2) twice, K 10] across to last 10 sts, K2, (P2, K2) twice.

Rows 14-17: Repeat Rows 10-13.

Row 18: Purl across.

Repeat Rows 1-18 for pattern.

68. TUMBLING BLOCKS

{10 x 24}

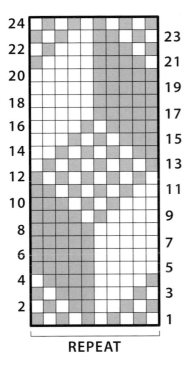

REPEAT

Row 1 (Right side): (K1, P1) across.

Row 2: [P1, K1, P1, K2, P2, K1, P1, K1) across.

Row 3: [K1, P1, K3, P3, K1, P1) across.

Row 4: [P1, K4, P4, K1) across.

Rows 5-8: [K5, P5] across.

Row 9: [K4, P1, K1, P4] across.

Row 10: [K3, (P1, K1) twice, P3] across.

Row 11: [K2, (P1, K1) 3 times, P2] across.

Row 12: [K1, P1] across.

Row 13: [P1, K1] across.

Row 14: [P2, (K1, P1) 3 times, K2] across.

Row 15: [P3, (K1, P1) twice, K3] across.

Row 16: [P4, K1, P1, K4] across.

Rows 17-20: [P5, K5] across.

Row 21: [K1, P4, K4, P1] across.

Row 22: [P1, K1, P3, K3, P1, K1] across.

Row 23: [K1, P1, K1, P2, K2, P1, K1, P1] across.

Row 24: [P1, K1] across.

Repeat Rows 1-24 for pattern.

69. IMITATION LATTICE

{12 + 1 x 24}

Row 1 (Right side)**:** [P4, K5, P3] across to last st, P1.

Row 2: K1, [K3, P5, K4] across.

Row 3: [P3, K3, P1, K3, P2] across to last st, P1.

Row 4: K1, [K2, P3, K1, P3, K3] across.

Row 5: [P2, K3, P3, K3, P1] across to last st, P1.

Row 6: K1, [K1, P3, K3, P3, K2] across.

Row 7: [P1, K3, P5, K3] across to last st, P1.

Row 8: K1, [P3, K5, P3, K1] across.

Row 9: [K3, P7, K2] across to last st, K1.

Row 10: P1, [P2, K7, P3] across.

Row 11: [K2, P9, K1] across to last st, K1.

Row 12: P1, [P1, K9, P2] across.

Rows 13 and 14: Repeat Rows 9 and 10.

Rows 15 and 16: Repeat Rows 7 and 8.

Rows 17 and 18: Repeat Rows 5 and 6.

Rows 19 and 20: Repeat Rows 3 and 4.

Rows 21 and 22: Repeat Rows 1 and 2.

Row 23: [P5, K3, P4] across to last st, P1.

Row 24: K1, [K4, P3, K5] across.

Repeat Rows 1-24 for pattern.

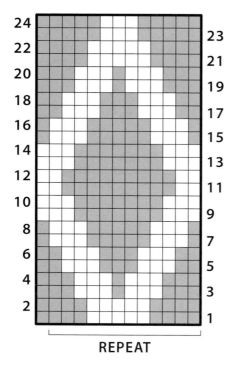

REPEAT

70. BOWTIES

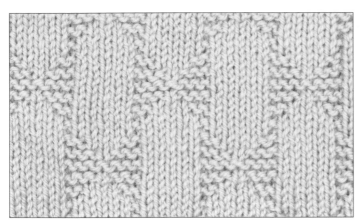

{12 + 1 x 24}

Row 1 (Right side)**:** [K3, P7, K2] across to last st, K1.

Row 2 AND ALL EVEN-NUMBERED ROWS: Purl across.

Row 3: [K3, P3, K1, P3, K2] across to last st, K1.

Row 5: [K3, P2, K3, P2, K2] across to last st, K1.

Row 7: [K3, P1, K5, P1, K2] across to last st, K1.

Row 9: [K2, P2, K5, P2, K1] across to last st, K1.

Row 11: [K1, P3, K5, P3] across to last st, K1.

Row 13: [P4, K5, P3] across to last st, P1.

Row 15: [K1, P3, K5, P3] across to last st, K1.

Row 17: [K2, P2, K5, P2, K1] across to last st, K1.

Row 19: [K3, P1, K5, P1, K2] across to last st, K1.

Row 21: [K3, P2, K3, P2, K2] across to last st, K1.

Row 23: [K3, P3, K1, P3, K2] across to last st, K1.

Row 24: Purl across.

Repeat Rows 1-24 for pattern.

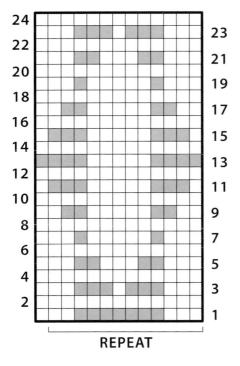

REPEAT

71. GARTER DIAMOND

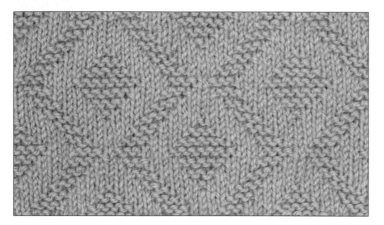

{20 + 1 x 24}

Row 1 (Right side)**:** [K1, P3, K3, P7, K3, P3] across to last st, K1.

Row 2 AND ALL EVEN-NUMBERED ROWS: Purl across.

Row 3: [K2, P3, K3, P5, K3, P3, K1] across to last st, K1.

Row 5: [(K3, P3) 3 times, K2] across to last st, K1.

Row 7: [P1, K3, P3, K3, P1, K3, P3, K3] across to last st, P1.

Row 9: [P2, K3, P3, K5, P3, K3, P1] across to last st, P1.

Row 11: [(P3, K3) 3 times, P2] across to last st, P1.

Row 13: [P4, K3, P3, K1, P3, K3, P3] across to last st, P1.

Row 15: Repeat Row 11.

Row 17: Repeat Row 9.

Row 19: Repeat Row 7.

Row 21: Repeat Row 5.

Row 23: Repeat Row 3.

Row 24: Purl across.

Repeat Rows 1-24 for pattern.

REPEAT

72. PATCHWORK

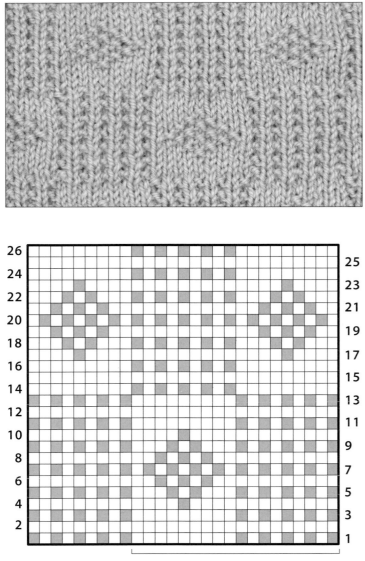

REPEAT

{18 + 9 x 26}

Row 1 (Right side)**:** [P1, (K1, P1) 4 times, K9] across to last 9 sts, P1, (K1, P1) 4 times.

Row 2: Purl across.

Row 3: Repeat Row 1.

Row 4: P9, [P4, K1, P 13] across.

Row 5: [P1, (K1, P1) 4 times, K3, P1, K1, P1, K3] across to last 9 sts, P1, (K1, P1) 4 times.

Row 6: P9, [P2, K1, (P1, K1) twice, P 11] across.

Row 7: [P1, K1] across to last st, P1.

Row 8: Repeat Row 6.

Row 9: Repeat Row 5.

Row 10: P9, [P4, K1, P 13] across.

Rows 11-13: Repeat Rows 1-3.

Row 14: P9, [K1, (P1, K1) 4 times, P9] across.

Row 15: Knit across.

Row 16: Repeat Row 14.

Row 17: [K4, P1, K 13] across to last 9 sts, K4, P1, K4.

Row 18: P3, K1, P1, K1, P3, [K1, (P1, K1) 4 times, P3, K1, P1, K1, P3] across.

Row 19: [K2, P1, (K1, P1) twice, K 11] across to last 9 sts, K2, P1, (K1, P1) twice, K2.

Row 20: P1, [K1, P1] across.

Row 21: Repeat Row 19.

Row 22: Repeat Row 18.

Row 23: Repeat Row 17.

Rows 24-26: Repeat Rows 14-16.

Repeat Rows 1-26 for pattern.

DISHCLOTHS

Nubby, reversible stitch patterns make great dishcloths!

◗■☐☐ **EASY**

MATERIALS

100% Cotton Medium Weight Yarn
[5 ounces, 236 yards
(140 grams, 212 meters) per ball]:
  One ball will make two Dishcloths
Straight knitting needles, size 6 (4 mm) **or** size needed for gauge
Markers

---

1. LITTLE PYRAMID (page 21)
Finished Size: 8½" (21.5 cm) square

GAUGE: In pattern,
18 sts and 30 rows = 4" (10 cm)

DISHCLOTH
Cast on 39 sts.

Row 1 (Right side)**:** Knit across.

Row 2: K2, place marker *(see Markers, page 139)*, knit across to last 2 sts, place marker, K2.

Work Little Pyramid pattern stitch, page 21, between markers keeping edge sts in Garter Stitch (knit each row) until piece measures approximately 8¼" (21 cm) from cast on edge, ending by working Row 6.

Last 2 Rows: Knit across, removing markers.

Bind off all sts in **knit**.

---

2. RIB AND WELT (page 39)
Finished Size: 8½" (21.5 cm) square

GAUGE: In pattern,
20 sts and 27 rows = 4" (10 cm)

DISHCLOTH
Cast on 44 sts.

Row 1 (Right side)**:** Knit across.

Row 2: K2, place marker *(see Markers, page 139)*, knit across to last 2 sts, place marker, K2.

Work Rib and Welt pattern stitch, page 39, between markers keeping edge sts in Garter Stitch (knit each row) until piece measures approximately 8¼" (21 cm) from cast on edge, ending by working Row 6.

Last 2 Rows: Knit across, removing markers.

Bind off all sts in **knit**.

---

3. SMALL BASKET (page 30)
Finished Size: 7¾" (19.5 cm) square

GAUGE: In pattern,
20 sts and 28 rows = 4" (10 cm)

DISHCLOTH
Cast on 39 sts.

Row 1 (Right side)**:** Knit across.

Row 2: K2, place marker *(see Markers, page 139)*, knit across to last 2 sts, place marker, K2.

Work Small Basket pattern stitch, page 30, between markers keeping edge sts in Garter Stitch (knit each row) until piece measures approximately 7½" (19 cm) from cast on edge, ending by working Row 4.

Last 2 Rows: Knit across, removing markers.

Bind off all sts in **knit**.

4. SMALL CHECKS (page 26)
Finished Size: 8¼" x 7¾" (21 cm x 19.5 cm)

GAUGE: In pattern, 18 sts and 27 rows = 4" (10 cm)

DISHCLOTH
Cast on 37 sts.

Row 1 (Right side)**:** Knit across.

Row 2: K2, place marker *(see Markers, page 139)*, knit across to last 2 sts, place marker, K2.

Work Small Checks pattern stitch, page 26, between markers keeping edge sts in Garter Stitch (knit each row) until piece measures approximately 7½" (19 cm) from cast on edge, ending by working Row 4 or Row 8.

Last 2 Rows: Knit across, removing markers.

Bind off all sts in **knit**.

5. KNITS AND PURLS (page 10)
Finished Size: 8" x 8¼" (20.5 cm x 21 cm)

GAUGE: In pattern, 18 sts and 30 rows = 4" (10 cm)

DISHCLOTH
Cast on 36 sts.

Work Knits and Purls pattern stitch, page 10, until piece measures approximately 8¼" (21 cm) from cast on edge, ending by working Row 1.

Bind off all sts in pattern.

6. MOSS AND RIB BLOCKS (page 38)
Finished Size: 7¼" x 7½" (18.5 cm x 19 cm)

GAUGE: In pattern, 19 sts and 24 rows = 4" (10 cm)

DISHCLOTH
Cast on 35 sts.

Row 1 (Right side)**:** Knit across.

Row 2: K2, place marker *(see Markers, page 139)*, knit across to last 2 sts, place marker, K2.

Work Moss and Rib Blocks pattern stitch, page 38, between markers keeping edge sts in Garter Stitch (knit each row) until piece measures approximately 7¼" (18.5 cm) from cast on edge, ending by working Row 6.

Last 2 Rows: Knit across, removing markers.

Bind off all sts in **knit**.

PILLOWS

Add texture to a living room or bedroom with lots of knit throw pillows!

Shown on page 53.

◀▪▪☐☐ **EASY**

MATERIALS

Medium Weight Yarn
[3 ounces, 197 yards
(85 grams, 180 meters) per ball]:
  3 balls for **each** Pillow
16" (40.5 cm) Square pillow form
Straight knitting needles, size 7 (4.5 mm) **or** size
  needed for gauge
Markers
Yarn needle

GAUGE: In Stockinette Stitch, 21 sts
      and 28 rows = 4" (10 cm)
Gauge will vary for each pattern
stitch used, and not all pieces will
measure exactly 16" (40.5 cm)
square. Fabric will stretch when
inserting pillow form.

BODY (Make 2)

Make 2 pieces of the Pattern Stitch
you desire on pages 51 and 52.

FINISHING

Weave seam on 3 sides *(Fig. 8, page 141)*. Insert pillow form and
weave remaining side closed.

PATTERN STITCHES

1. GARTER DIAMOND (page 46)

Cast on 83 sts.

Row 1 (Wrong side)**:** P1, place
marker *(see Markers, page 139)*,
purl across to last st, place marker,
P1.

Work Rows 1-24 of Garter Diamond
pattern stitch, page 46, between
markers keeping edge sts in
Stockinette Stitch (knit on right
side rows, purl on wrong side rows)
until piece measures approximately
16" (40.5 cm) from cast on edge,
ending by working a **wrong** side
row.

Bind off all sts in **knit**.

2. TUMBLING BLOCKS (page 43)

Cast on 82 sts.

Row 1 (Wrong side)**:** P1, place
marker *(see Markers, page 139)*,
purl across to last st, place marker,
P1.

Work Rows 1-24 of Tumbling
Blocks pattern stitch, page 43,
between markers keeping edge sts
in Stockinette Stitch (knit on right
side rows, purl on wrong side rows)
until piece measures approximately
16" (40.5 cm) from cast on edge,
ending by working a **wrong** side
row.

Bind off all sts in **knit**.

3. DIAGONALS (page 30)
Cast on 82 sts.

Row 1 (Wrong side)**:** P2, place marker *(see Markers, page 139)*, purl across to last 2 sts, place marker, P2.

Work Rows 1-8 of Diagonals pattern stitch, page 30, between markers keeping edge sts in Stockinette Stitch (knit on right side rows, purl on wrong side rows) until piece measures approximately 16" (40.5 cm) from cast on edge, ending by working a **wrong** side row.

Bind off all sts in **knit**.

4. IMITATION LATTICE (page 44)
Cast on 79 sts.

Row 1 (Wrong side)**:** P3, place marker *(see Markers, page 139)*, purl across to last 3 sts, place marker, P3.

Work Rows 1-24 of Imitation Lattice pattern stitch, page 44, between markers keeping edge sts in Stockinette Stitch (knit on right side rows, purl on wrong side rows) until piece measures approximately 16" (40.5 cm) from cast on edge, ending by working a **wrong** side row.

Bind off all sts in **knit**.

5. PATCHWORK (page 47)
Cast on 83 sts.

Row 1 (Wrong side)**:** P1, place marker *(see Markers, page 139)*, purl across to last st, place marker, P1.

Work Rows 1-26 of Patchwork pattern stitch, page 47, between markers keeping edge sts in Stockinette Stitch (knit on right side rows, purl on wrong side rows) until piece measures approximately 16" (40.5 cm) from cast on edge, ending by working a **wrong** side row.

Bind off all sts in **knit**.

6. DOUBLE BASKET (page 42)
Cast on 84 sts.

Row 1 (Wrong side)**:** P1, place marker *(see Markers, page 139)*, purl across to last st, place marker, P1.

Work Rows 1-18 of Double Basket pattern stitch, page 42, between markers keeping edge sts in Stockinette Stitch (knit on right side rows, purl on wrong side rows) until piece measures approximately 16" (40.5 cm) from cast on edge, ending by working a **wrong** side row.

Bind off all sts in **knit**.

7. FANCY TRACK (page 31)
Cast on 79 sts.

Row 1 (Wrong side)**:** P3, place marker *(see Markers, page 139)*, purl across to last 3 sts, place marker, P3.

Work Rows 1-8 of Fancy Track pattern stitch, page 31, between markers keeping edge sts in Stockinette Stitch (knit on right side rows, purl on wrong side rows) until piece measures approximately 16" (40.5 cm) from cast on edge, ending by working a **wrong** side row.

Bind off all sts in **knit**.

8. PINNACLE CHEVRON (page 41)
Cast on 93 sts.

Row 1 (Wrong side)**:** P1, place marker *(see Markers, page 139)*, purl across to last st, place marker, P1.

Work Rows 1-16 of Pinnacle Chevron pattern stitch, page 41, between markers keeping edge sts in Stockinette Stitch (knit on right side rows, purl on wrong side rows) until piece measures approximately 16" (40.5 cm) from cast on edge, ending by working a **wrong** side row.

Bind off all sts in **knit**.

SAMPLER THROW

What a warm, lovely way to learn a variety of pattern stitches!

◼◼☐☐ EASY

Finished Size:
51" x 65" (129.5 cm x 165 cm)

MATERIALS

Medium Weight Yarn
[3.5 ounces, 200 yards
(100 grams, 183 meters) per ball]:
Color A (Ecru) - 3 balls
Color B (Purple) - 2 balls
Color C (Aran)- 3 balls
Color D (Green) - 2 balls
Color E (Mint) - 2 balls
Color F (BLue) - 2 balls
Color G (Beige) - 2 balls
Color H (Dk Beige) - 3 balls
Straight knitting needles, size 7
(4.5 mm) **or** size needed for
gauge
29" (73.5 cm) Circular knitting
needles, size 7 (4.5 mm)
Markers
Yarn needle

GAUGE: In Stockinette Stitch, 21 sts
and 28 rows = 4" (10 cm)
Gauge will vary for each pattern
stitch used.
Extra stitches and/or rows have
been added to some of the Blocks
so that each Block is approximately
7" (18 cm) square.

BODY

BLOCKS 1 & 49 - Double Moss, page 16
With Color A, cast on 38 sts.

Row 1 (Wrong side)**:** Purl across.

Work Double Moss pattern stitch,
page 16, until Block measures
approximately 7" (18 cm) from
cast on edge, ending by working a
wrong side row.

Bind off all sts in **knit**.

BLOCK 2 - Little Arrows, page 18
With Color B, cast on 37 sts.

Row 1 (Wrong side)**:** P2, place
marker (**see Markers, page 139**),
purl across to last 2 sts, place
marker, P2.

Work Little Arrows pattern stitch,
page 18, between markers keeping
edge sts in Stockinette Stitch (knit
on right side rows, purl on wrong
side rows) until Block measures
approximately 7" (18 cm) from cast
on edge, ending by working Row 4.

Bind off all sts in **knit**.

BLOCK 3 - King Charles, page 37
With Color C, cast on 37 sts.

Row 1 (Wrong side)**:** Purl across.

Work King Charles pattern stitch,
page 37, until Block measures
approximately 7" (18 cm) from
cast on edge, ending by working
Row 12.

Bind off all sts in **knit**.

BLOCK 4 - Triangle Rib, page 17
With Color F, cast on 37 sts.

Row 1 (Wrong side)**:** K2, place
marker (**see Markers, page 139**),
purl across to last 2 sts, place
marker, K2.

Work Triangle Rib pattern stitch,
page 17, between markers keeping
edge sts in Garter Stitch (knit
each row) until Block measures
approximately 7" (18 cm) from cast
on edge, ending by working Row 4.

Bind off all sts in **knit**.

Instructions continued on page 56.

BLOCK 5 - Lattice, page 20
With Color A, cast on 37 sts.

Row 1 (Wrong side)**:** Purl across.

Work Lattice pattern stitch, page 20, until Block measures approximately 7" (18 cm) from cast on edge, ending by working Row 6.

Bind off all sts in **knit**.

BLOCK 6 - Moss, page 14
With Color B, cast on 37 sts.

Row 1 (Wrong side)**:** Purl across.

Work Moss pattern stitch, page 14, until Block measures approximately 7" (18 cm) from cast on edge, ending by working Row 4.

Bind off all sts in **knit**.

BLOCK 7 - Flame, page 40
With Color C, cast on 38 sts.

Row 1 (Wrong side)**:** K3, place marker (*see Markers, page 139*), purl across to last 3 sts, place marker, K3.

Work Flame pattern stitch, page 40, between markers keeping edge sts in Garter Stitch (knit each row) until Block measures approximately 7" (18 cm) from cast on edge, ending by working Row 8 or Row 16.

Bind off all sts in **knit**.

BLOCKS 8 & 28 - Knit and Rib, page 33
With Color D, cast on 38 sts.

Row 1 (Wrong side)**:** P1, place marker (*see Markers, page 139*), purl across to last st, place marker, P1.

Work Knit and Rib pattern stitch, page 33, between markers keeping edge sts in Stockinette Stitch (knit on right side rows, purl on wrong side rows) until Block measures approximately 7" (18 cm) from cast on edge, ending by working Row 1 or Row 7.

Bind off all sts in **knit**.

BLOCK 9 - Diamond Brocade, page 28
With Color G, cast on 37 sts.

Row 1 (Wrong side)**:** K2, place marker (*see Markers, page 139*), purl across to last 2 sts, place marker, K2.

Work Diamond Brocade pattern stitch, page 28, between markers keeping edge sts in Garter Stitch (knit each row) until Block measures approximately 7" (18 cm) from cast on edge, ending by working Row 8.

Bind off all sts in **knit**.

BLOCK 10 - Embossed, page 24
With Color E, cast on 37 sts.

Row 1 (Wrong side)**:** Purl across.

Work Embossed pattern stitch, page 24, until Block measures approximately 7" (18 cm) from cast on edge, ending by working Row 8.

Bind off all sts in **knit**.

BLOCK 11 - Zigzag Rib, page 19
With Color H, cast on 41 sts.

Row 1 (Wrong side)**:** Purl across.

Work Zigzag Rib pattern stitch, page 19, until Block measures approximately 7" (18 cm) from cast on edge, ending by working Row 4.

Bind off all sts in **knit**.

BLOCK 12 - Moss Rib, page 23
With Color D, cast on 37 sts.

Row 1 (Wrong side)**:** K2, place marker (*see Markers, page 139*), purl across to last 2 sts, place marker, K2.

Work Moss Rib pattern stitch, page 23, between markers keeping edge sts in Garter Stitch (knit each row) until Block measures approximately 7" (18 cm) from cast on edge, ending by working Row 6.

Bind off all sts in **knit**.

BLOCK 13 - Vertical Parallelograms, page 25
With Color G, cast on 37 sts.

Row 1 (Wrong side)**:** P1, place marker (*see Markers, page 139*), purl across to last st, place marker, P1.

Work Vertical Parallelograms pattern stitch, page 25, between markers keeping edge sts in Stockinette Stitch (knit on right side rows, purl on wrong side rows) until Block measures approximately 7" (18 cm) from cast on edge, ending by working Row 8.

Bind off all sts in **knit**.

BLOCK 14 - Basket Weave, page 23

With Color E, cast on 38 sts.

Row 1 (Wrong side): K2, place marker (*see Markers, page 139*), purl across to last 2 sts, place marker, K2.

Work Basket Weave pattern stitch, page 23, between markers keeping edge sts in Garter Stitch (knit each row) until Block measures approximately 7" (18 cm) from cast on edge, ending by working Row 6.

Bind off all sts in **knit**.

BLOCK 15 - Scales, page 37

With Color C, cast on 38 sts.

Row 1 (Wrong side): P1, place marker (*see Markers, page 139*), purl across to last st, place marker, P1.

Work Scales pattern stitch, page 37, between markers keeping edge sts in Stockinette Stitch (knit on right side rows, purl on wrong side rows) until Block measures approximately 7" (18 cm) from cast on edge, ending by working Row 12.

Bind off all sts in **knit**.

BLOCK 16 - Little Pyramid, page 21

With Color F, cast on 37 sts.

Row 1 (Wrong side): K1, place marker (*see Markers, page 139*), purl across to last st, place marker, K1.

Work Little Pyramid pattern stitch, page 21, between markers keeping edge sts in Garter Stitch (knit each row) until Block measures approximately 7" (18 cm) from cast on edge, ending by working Row 3 or Row 6.

Bind off all sts in **knit**.

BLOCK 17 - Rib and Diamond, page 38

With Color A, cast on 43 sts.

Row 1 (Wrong side): Purl across.

Work Rib and Diamond pattern stitch, page 38, until Block measures approximately 7" (18 cm) from cast on edge, ending by working Row 12.

Bind off all sts in **knit**.

BLOCK 18 - Seed, page 8

With Color B, cast on 35 sts.

Row 1 (Wrong side): Purl across.

Work Seed pattern stitch, page 8, until Block measures approximately 7" (18 cm) from cast on edge, ending by working a **wrong** side row.

Bind off all sts in **knit**.

BLOCK 19 - Moss Diamonds, page 36

With Color C, cast on 39 sts.

Row 1 (Wrong side): P1, place marker (*see Markers, page 139*), purl across to last st, place marker, P1.

Work Moss Diamonds pattern stitch, page 36, between markers keeping edge sts in Stockinette Stitch (knit on right side rows, purl on wrong side rows) until Block measures approximately 7" (18 cm) from cast on edge, ending by working Row 6 or Row 12.

Bind off all sts in **knit**.

BLOCK 20 - Simple Texture, page 15

With Color F, cast on 37 sts.

Row 1 (Wrong side): Purl across.

Work Simple Texture pattern stitch, page 15, until Block measures approximately 7" (18 cm) from cast on edge, ending by working a **wrong** side row.

Bind off all sts in **knit**.

BLOCK 21 - Garter Zigzag, page 33

With Color A, cast on 36 sts.

Row 1 (Wrong side): Purl across.

Work Garter Zigzag pattern stitch, page 33, until Block measures approximately 7" (18 cm) from cast on edge, ending by working Row 6 or Row 12.

Bind off all sts in **knit**.

Instructions continued on page 58.

BLOCK 22 - Modified Seed, page 13

With Color E, cast on 38 sts.

Row 1 (Wrong side): Purl across.

Work Modified Seed pattern stitch, page 13, until Block measures approximately 7" (18 cm) from cast on edge, ending by working a **wrong** side row.

Bind off all sts in **knit**.

BLOCK 23 - Open Chevron, page 18

With Color H, cast on 37 sts.

Row 1 (Wrong side): K2, place marker *(see Markers, page 139)*, purl across to last 2 sts, place marker, K2.

Work Open Chevron pattern stitch, page 18, between markers keeping edge sts in Garter Stitch (knit each row) until Block measures approximately 7" (18 cm) from cast on edge, ending by working Row 4.

Bind off all sts in **knit**.

BLOCK 24 - Fancy Track, page 31

With Color D, cast on 37 sts.

Row 1 (Wrong side): Purl across.

Work Fancy Track pattern stitch, page 31, until Block measures approximately 7" (18 cm) from cast on edge, ending by working Row 4 or Row 8.

Bind off all sts in **knit**.

BLOCK 25 - Garter Check, page 39

With Color G, cast on 35 sts.

Row 1 (Wrong side): K1, place marker *(see Markers, page 139)*, purl across to last st, place marker, K1.

Work Garter Check pattern stitch, page 39, between markers keeping edge sts in Garter Stitch (knit each row) until Block measures approximately 7" (18 cm) from cast on edge, ending by working Row 8 or Row 16.

Bind off all sts in **knit**.

BLOCK 26 - Little Arrows, page 18

With Color E, work same as Block 2, page 54.

BLOCK 27 - Reverse Stocking Chevrons, page 21

With Color H, cast on 37 sts.

Row 1 (Wrong side): P1, place marker *(see Markers, page 139)*, purl across to last st, place marker, P1.

Work Reverse Stocking Chevrons pattern stitch, page 21, between markers keeping edge sts in Stockinette Stitch (knit on right side rows, purl on wrong side rows) until Block measures approximately 7" (18 cm) from cast on edge, ending by working Row 6.

Bind off all sts in **knit**.

BLOCK 29 - Single Basket Weave, page 20

With Color A, cast on 42 sts.

Row 1 (Wrong side): K2, place marker *(see Markers, page 139)*, purl across to last 2 sts, place marker, K2.

Work Single Basket Weave pattern stitch, page 20, between markers keeping edge sts in Garter Stitch (knit each row) until Block measures approximately 7" (18 cm) from cast on edge, ending by working Row 6.

Bind off all sts in **knit**.

BLOCK 30 - King Charles, page 37

With Color B, work same as Block 3, page 54.

BLOCK 31 - Mirrored Triangle, page 34

With Color C, cast on 37 sts.

Row 1 (Wrong side): P1, place marker *(see Markers, page 139)*, purl across to last st, place marker, P1.

Work Mirrored Triangle pattern stitch, page 34, between markers keeping edge sts in Stockinette Stitch (knit on right side rows, purl on wrong side rows) until Block measures approximately 7" (18 cm) from cast on edge, ending by working Row 6 or Row 12.

Bind off all sts in **knit**.

Instructions continued on page 60.

BLOCK 32 - Diamond Panels, page 28

With Color F, cast on 37 sts.

Row 1 (Wrong side)**:** K2, place marker *(see Markers, page 139)*, purl across to last 2 sts, place marker, K2.

Work Diamond Panels pattern stitch, page 28, between markers keeping edge sts in Garter Stitch (knit each row) until Block measures approximately 7" (18 cm) from cast on edge, ending by working Row 8.

Bind off all sts in **knit**.

BLOCK 33 - 3 and 1, page 15

With Color A, cast on 37 sts.

Row 1 (Wrong side)**:** K2, place marker *(see Markers, page 139)*, purl across to last 2 sts, place marker, K2.

Work 3 and 1 pattern stitch, page 15, between markers keeping edge sts in Garter Stitch (knit each row) until Block measures approximately 7" (18 cm) from cast on edge, ending by working Row 4.

Bind off all sts in **knit**.

BLOCK 34 - Lozenge, page 36

With Color B, cast on 37 sts.

Row 1 (Wrong side)**:** K2, place marker *(see Markers, page 139)*, purl across to last 2 sts, place marker, K2.

Work Lozenge pattern stitch, page 36, between markers keeping edge sts in Garter Stitch (knit each row) until Block measures approximately 7" (18 cm) from cast on edge, ending by working Row 6 or Row 12.

Bind off all sts in **knit**.

BLOCK 35 - Petite Seed Diamonds, page 32

With Color C, cast on 38 sts.

Row 1 (Wrong side)**:** P1, place marker *(see Markers, page 139)*, purl across to last st, place marker, P1.

Work Petite Seed Diamonds pattern stitch, page 32, between markers keeping edge sts in Stockinette Stitch (knit on right side rows, purl on wrong side rows) until Block measures approximately 7" (18 cm) from cast on edge, ending by working Row 6 or Row 12.

Bind off all sts in **knit**.

BLOCK 36 - Swedish Block, page 26

With Color D, cast on 38 sts.

Row 1 (Wrong side)**:** Purl across.

Work Swedish Block pattern stitch, page 26, until Block measures approximately 7" (18 cm) from cast on edge, ending by working Row 4 or Row 8.

Bind off all sts in **knit**.

BLOCK 37 - Garter Stitch, page 8

With Color G, cast on 36 sts.

Row 1 (Wrong side)**:** Purl across.

Work Garter Stitch pattern stitch, page 8, until Block measures approximately 7" (18 cm) from cast on edge, ending by working a **wrong** side row.

Bind off all sts in **knit**.

BLOCK 38 - Bowties, page 45

With Color E, cast on 37 sts.

Row 1 (Wrong side)**:** Purl across.

Work Bowties pattern stitch, page 45, until Block measures approximately 7" (18 cm) from cast on edge, ending by working Row 24.

Bind off all sts in **knit**.

BLOCK 39 - Double Moss Rib, page 16

With Color H, cast on 41 sts.

Row 1 (Wrong side)**:** K2, place marker *(see Markers, page 139)*, purl across to last 2 sts, place marker, K2.

Work Double Moss Rib pattern stitch, page 16, between markers keeping edge sts in Garter Stitch (knit each row) until Block measures approximately 7" (18 cm) from cast on edge, ending by working Row 4.

Bind off all sts in **knit**.

BLOCK 40 - Little Knot, page 27

With Color D, cast on 37 sts.

Row 1 (Wrong side)**:** K2, place marker *(see Markers, page 139)*, purl across to last 2 sts, place marker, K2.

Work Little Knot pattern stitch, page 27, between markers keeping edge sts in Garter Stitch (knit each row) until Block measures approximately 7" (18 cm) from cast on edge, ending by working Row 4 or Row 8.

Bind off all sts in **knit**.

BLOCK 41 - Reverse Stocking Chevrons, page 21

With Color G, work same as Block 27, page 58.

BLOCK 42 - Sugar Cubes, page 27

With Color E, cast on 37 sts.

Row 1 (Wrong side)**:** K2, place marker *(see Markers, page 139)*, purl across to last 2 sts, place marker, K2.

Work Sugar Cubes pattern stitch, page 27, between markers keeping edge sts in Garter Stitch (knit each row) until Block measures approximately 7" (18 cm) from cast on edge, ending by working Row 4 or Row 8.

Bind off all sts in **knit**.

BLOCK 43 - Diagonals, page 30

With Color C, cast on 38 sts.

Row 1 (Wrong side)**:** Purl across.

Work Diagonals pattern stitch, page 30, until Block measures approximately 7" (18 cm) from cast on edge, ending by working Row 8.

Bind off all sts in **knit**.

BLOCK 44 - Lozenge, page 36

With Color F, work same as Block 34, page 60.

BLOCK 45 - Seed, page 8

With Color A, work same as Block 18, page 57.

BLOCK 46 - Broken Rib, page 9

With Color B, cast on 37 sts.

Row 1 (Wrong side)**:** Purl across.

Work Broken Rib pattern stitch, page 9, until Block measures approximately 7" (18 cm) from cast on edge, ending by working a **wrong** side row.

Bind off all sts in **knit**.

BLOCK 47 - Ripple Stripe, page 22

With Color C, cast on 37 sts.

Row 1 (Wrong side)**:** K2, place marker *(see Markers, page 139)*, purl across to last 2 sts, place marker, K2.

Work Ripple Stripe pattern stitch, page 22, between markers keeping edge sts in Garter Stitch (knit each row) until Block measures approximately 7" (18 cm) from cast on edge, ending by working Row 6.

Bind off all sts in **knit**.

Instructions continued on page 62.

BLOCK 48 - Moss Diamonds, page 36
With Color F, cast on 41 sts.

Row 1 (Wrong side)**:** K2, place marker (*see Markers, page 139*), purl across to last 2 sts, place marker, K2.

Work Moss Diamonds pattern stitch, page 36, between markers keeping edge sts in Garter Stitch (knit each row) until Block measures approximately 7" (18 cm) from cast on edge, ending by working Row 12.

Bind off all sts in **knit**.

BLOCK 50 - Double Fleck, page 17
With Color E, cast on 36 sts.

Row 1 (Wrong side)**:** P1, place marker (*see Markers, page 139*), purl across to last st, place marker, P1.

Work Double Fleck pattern stitch, page 17, between markers keeping edge sts in Stockinette Stitch (knit on right side rows, purl on wrong side rows) until Block measures approximately 7" (18 cm) from cast on edge, ending by working Row 4.

Bind off all sts in **knit**.

BLOCK 51- Little Knot, page 27
With Color H, work same as Block 40, page 61.

BLOCK 52 - Sand, page 10
With Color D, cast on 37 sts.

Row 1 (Wrong side)**:** Purl across.

Work Sand pattern stitch, page 10, until Block measures approximately 7" (18 cm) from cast on edge, ending by working a **wrong** side row.

Bind off all sts in **knit**.

BLOCK 53 - Small Checks, page 26
With Color G, cast on 37 sts.

Row 1 (Wrong side)**:** K2, place marker (*see Markers, page 139*), purl across to last 2 sts, place marker, K2.

Work Small Checks pattern stitch, page 26, between markers keeping edge sts in Garter Stitch (knit each row) until Block measures approximately 7" (18 cm) from cast on edge, ending by working Row 4 or Row 8.

Bind off all sts in **knit**.

BLOCK 54 - Diamonds and Purls, page 29
With Color E, cast on 37 sts.

Row 1 (Wrong side)**:** K2, place marker (*see Markers, page 139*), purl across to last 2 sts, place marker, K2.

Work Diamonds and Purls pattern stitch, page 29, between markers keeping edge sts in Garter Stitch (knit each row) until Block measures approximately 7" (18 cm) from cast on edge, ending by working Row 8.

Bind off all sts in **knit**.

BLOCK 55 - Basket Weave Rib, page 35
With Color H, cast on 37 sts.

Row 1 (Wrong side)**:** K2, place marker (*see Markers, page 139*), purl across to last 2 sts, place marker, K2.

Work Basket Weave Rib pattern stitch, page 35, between markers keeping edge sts in Garter Stitch (knit each row) until Block measures approximately 7" (18 cm) from cast on edge, ending by working Row 6 or Row 12.

Bind off all sts in **knit**.

BLOCK 56 - Moss Zigzag, page 31
With Color D, cast on 38 sts.

Row 1 (Wrong side)**:** P1, place marker *(see Markers, page 139)*, purl across to last st, place marker, P1.

Work Moss Zigzag pattern stitch, page 31, between markers keeping edge sts in Stockinette Stitch (knit on right side rows, purl on wrong side rows) until Block measures approximately 7" (18 cm) from cast on edge, ending by working Row 10.

Bind off all sts in **knit**.

BLOCK 57 - Baby Weave, page 25
With Color A, cast on 40 sts.

Row 1 (Wrong side)**:** P1, place marker *(see Markers, page 139)*, purl across to last st, place marker, P1.

Work Baby Weave pattern stitch, page 25, between markers keeping edge sts in Stockinette Stitch (knit on right side rows, purl on wrong side rows) until Block measures approximately 7" (18 cm) from cast on edge, ending by working Row 4 or Row 8.

Bind off all sts in **knit**.

BLOCK 58 - Ladder, page 22
With Color B, cast on 37 sts.

Row 1 (Wrong side)**:** P1, place marker *(see Markers, page 139)*, purl across to last st, place marker, P1.

Work Ladder pattern stitch, page 22, between markers keeping edge sts in Stockinette Stitch (knit on right side rows, purl on wrong side rows) until Block measures approximately 7" (18 cm) from cast on edge, ending by working Row 6.

Bind off all sts in **knit**.

BLOCK 59 - Wave, page 19
With Color C, cast on 37 sts.

Row 1 (Wrong side)**:** Purl across.

Work Wave pattern stitch, page 19, until Block measures approximately 7" (18 cm) from cast on edge, ending by working Row 4.

Bind off all sts in **knit**.

BLOCK 60 - Garter Stitch Columns, page 35
With Color F, cast on 37 sts.

Row 1 (Wrong side)**:** K2, place marker *(see Markers, page 139)*, purl across to last 2 sts, place marker, K2.

Work Garter Stitch Columns pattern stitch, page 35, between markers keeping edge sts in Garter Stitch (knit each row) until Block measures approximately 7" (18 cm) from cast on edge, ending by working Row 12.

Bind off all sts in **knit**.

BLOCK 61- Waffle Sitch, page 14
With Color A, cast on 44 sts.

Row 1 (Wrong side)**:** K2, place marker *(see Markers, page 139)*, purl across to last 2 sts, place marker, K2.

Work Waffle Stitch pattern stitch, page 14, between markers keeping edge sts in Garter Stitch (knit each row) until Block measures approximately 7" (18 cm) from cast on edge, ending by working Row 4.

Bind off all sts in **knit**.

Instructions continued on page 64.

BLOCK 62 - Woven Squares, page 32

With Color B, cast on 39 sts.

Row 1 (Wrong side)**:** Purl across.

Work Woven Squares pattern stitch, page 32, until Block measures approximately 7" (18 cm) from cast on edge, ending by working Row 10.

Bind off all sts in **knit**.

BLOCK 63 - Diagonal Rib, page 24

With Color C, cast on 38 sts.

Row 1 (Wrong side)**:** P1, place marker *(see Markers, page 139)*, purl across to last st, place marker, P1.

Work Diagonal Rib pattern stitch, page 24, between markers keeping edge sts in Stockinette Stitch (knit on right side rows, purl on wrong side rows) until Block measures approximately 7" (18 cm) from cast on edge, ending by working Row 8.

Bind off all sts in **knit**.

FINISHING
BLOCKING

Block pieces to measure 7" (18 cm) square as follows:
Place the item to be blocked on a clean terry towel over a flat surface and shape; pin in place using rust-proof pins where needed. Hold a steam iron or steamer just above the item and steam it thoroughly. Never let the weight of the iron touch the item because it will flatten the stitches. Leave the item pinned until it is completely dry.

ASSEMBLY

Using Placement Diagram as a guide and matching color, sew Blocks together, forming 9 horizontal strips of 7 Blocks each; then sew strips together.

SIDE BORDER

With **right** side of long edge facing, using circular needle, and Color H, pick up 37 sts across each Block *(Figs. 7a & b, page 141)*: 333 sts.

Row 1: Knit across.

Row 2: K1, (P1, K1) across.

Rows 3-5: Repeat Rows 1 and 2 once, then repeat Row 1 once **more**.

Bind off all sts in **knit**.

Repeat along second long edge.

TOP BORDER

With **right** side of short edge facing, using circular needle, and Color H, pick up 4 sts across Side Border; pick up 37 sts across each Block; pick up 4 sts across Side Border: 267 sts.

Complete same as Side Border.

Repeat across second short edge.

1	2	3	4	5	6	7
8	9	10	11	12	13	14
15	16	17	18	19	20	21
22	23	24	25	26	27	28
29	30	31	32	33	34	35
36	37	38	39	40	41	42
43	44	45	46	47	48	49
50	51	52	53	54	55	56
57	58	59	60	61	62	63

GARTER DIAMOND THROW

A cozy gift for a loved one, or a sweet treat for yourself—these diamonds will be anybody's best friend!

EASY

Finished Size: 46" x 62" (117 cm x 157.5 cm)

MATERIALS

Bulky Weight Yarn
[3.5 ounces, 148 yards
(100 grams, 136 meters) per ball]:
15 balls
29" (73.5 cm) Circular knitting,
needle size 10 (6 mm) **or** size
needed for gauge

GAUGE: In pattern
(Garter Diamonds,
page 46),
20 sts = 5½" (14 cm);
24 rows = 4" (10 cm)

BOTTOM BORDER
Cast on 171 sts.
Rows 1-5: Knit across (Garter Stitch).

BODY
Row 1 (Right side)**:** K6, P3, K3, P7, K3, P3, ★ K1, P3, K3, P7, K3, P3; repeat from ★ across to last 6 sts, K6.

Row 2 AND ALL WRONG SIDE ROWS: K5, purl across to last 5 sts, K5.

Row 3: K7, P3, K3, P5, ★ K3, (P3, K3) twice, P5; repeat from ★ across to last 13 sts, K3, P3, K7.

Row 5: K8, P3, (K3, P3) twice, ★ K5, P3, (K3, P3) twice; repeat from ★ across to last 8 sts, K8.

Row 7: K5, P1, ★ K3, P3, K3, P1; repeat from ★ across to last 5 sts, K5.

Row 9: K5, P2, K3, P3, K5, ★ P3, (K3, P3) twice, K5; repeat from ★ across to last 13 sts, P3, K3, P2, K5.

Row 11: K5, (P3, K3) 3 times, ★ P5, K3, (P3, K3) twice; repeat from ★ across to last 8 sts, P3, K5.

Row 13: K5, P4, K3, P3, K1, P3, K3, ★ P7, K3, P3, K1, P3, K3; repeat from ★ across to last 9 sts, P4, K5.

Row 15: Repeat Row 11.

Row 17: Repeat Row 9.

Row 19: Repeat Row 7.

Row 21: Repeat Row 5.

Row 23: Repeat Row 3.

Row 24: K5, purl across to last 5 sts, K5.

Rows 25-360: Repeat Rows 1-24, 14 times.

TOP BORDER
Rows 1-5: Knit across.

Bind off all sts in **knit**.

TUMBLING BLOCKS BABY BLANKET

Little fingers will enjoy exploring these geometric textures.
The pattern is simple to knit and the blanket is easy to love!

Finished Size: 36" (91.5 cm) square

MATERIALS

Medium Weight Yarn
[3.5 ounces, 178 yards
(100 grams, 163 meters) per
skein]: 6 skeins
29" (73.5 cm) Circular knitting
needle, size 10 (6 mm) **or** size
needed for gauge

GAUGE: In pattern
(Tumbling Blocks,
page 43), 19 sts and
28 rows = 4" (10 cm)

BOTTOM BORDER
Cast on 172 sts.

Row 1: (P1, K1) across

Row 2: (K1, P1) across.

Rows 3-7: Repeat Rows 1 and 2
twice, then repeat Row 1 once
more.

BODY
Row 1 (Right side)**:** (K1, P1) across.

Row 2: P1, (K1, P1) 4 times, K2, P2, ★
(K1, P1) 3 times, K2, P2; repeat from
★ across to last 9 sts, K1, (P1, K1) 4
times.

Row 3: (K1, P1) 4 times, K3, P3,
★ (K1, P1) twice, K3, P3; repeat
from ★ across to last 8 sts, (K1, P1)
4 times.

Row 4: P1, (K1, P1) 3 times, K4, P4,
K1, ★ P1, K4, P4, K1; repeat from ★
across to last 6 sts, (P1, K1) 3 times.

Row 5: (K1, P1) 3 times, (K5, P5)
across to last 6 sts, (K1, P1) 3 times.

Row 6: P1, (K1, P1) twice, K6,
(P5, K5) across to last 11 sts, P6, K1,
(P1, K1) twice.

Rows 7 and 8: Repeat Rows 5
and 6.

Row 9: (K1, P1) 3 times, ★ K4, P1,
K1, P4; repeat from ★ across to last
6 sts, (K1, P1) 3 times.

Row 10: P1, (K1, P1) twice, K4, (P1,
K1) twice, ★ P3, K3, (P1, K1) twice;
repeat from ★ across to last 9 sts,
P4, K1, (P1, K1) twice.

Row 11: (K1, P1) 3 times, ★ K2, (P1,
K1) 3 times, P2; repeat from ★ across
to last 6 sts, (K1, P1)
3 times.

Row 12: P1, (K1, P1) twice, K2, (P1,
K1) across to last 7 sts, P2, K1, (P1,
K1) twice.

Row 13: K1, (P1, K1) twice, P2, (K1,
P1) across to last 7 sts, K2, P1, (K1,
P1) twice.

Row 14: (P1, K1) 3 times, ★ P2, (K1,
P1) 3 times, K2; repeat from ★ across
to last 6 sts, (P1, K1)
3 times.

Row 15: K1, (P1, K1) twice, P4, (K1,
P1) twice, ★ K3, P3, (K1, P1) twice;
repeat from ★ across to last 9 sts,
K4, P1, (K1, P1) twice.

Row 16: (P1, K1) 3 times, ★ P4, K1,
P1, K4; repeat from ★ across to last
6 sts, (P1, K1) 3 times.

Row 17: K1, (P1, K1) twice, P6, (K5,
P5) across to last 11 sts, K6, P1, (K1,
P1) twice.

Row 18: (P1, K1) 3 times, (P5, K5) across to last 6 sts, (P1, K1) 3 times.

Rows 19 and 20: Repeat Rows 17 and 18.

Row 21: K1, (P1, K1) 3 times, P4, K4, P1, (K1, P4, K4, P1) across to last 6 sts, (K1, P1) 3 times.

Row 22: (P1, K1) 4 times, P3, K3, ★ (P1, K1) twice, P3, K3; repeat from ★ across to last 8 sts, (P1, K1) 4 times.

Row 23: K1, (P1, K1) 4 times, P2, K2, ★ (P1, K1) 3 times, P2, K2; repeat from ★ across to last 9 sts, P1, (K1, P1) 4 times.

Row 24: (P1, K1) across.

Rows 25-240: Repeat Rows 1-24, 9 times.

TOP BORDER

Row 1: (K1, P1) across.

Row 2: (P1, K1) across.

Rows 3-7: Repeat Rows 1 and 2 twice, then repeat Row 1 once **more**.

Bind off all sts in pattern.

SUGAR CUBE SHELL

Just enough textural interest to make it fun!
If you don't want the bottom edge ribbed, try the double moss stitch pattern, page 13, in its place.

◼◼◻◻ **EASY**

Size	Finished Chest Measurement	
Extra Small	32"	(81.5 cm)
Small	37¼"	(94.5 cm)
Medium	40"	(101.5 cm)
Large	45¼"	(115 cm)
Extra Large	48"	(122 cm)
2X-Large	53¼"	(135.5 cm)
3X-Large	56"	(142 cm)
4X-Large	61¼"	(155.5 cm)

Size Note: Instructions are written with sizes Extra Small and Small in the first set of braces { }, sizes Medium, Large, and Extra Large in the second set of braces, and sizes 2X-Large, 3X-Large, and 4X-Large in the third set of braces. Instructions will be easier to read if you circle all the numbers pertaining to your size. If only one number is given, it applies to all sizes.

MATERIALS

LIGHT 3

Light Weight Yarn
[2.5 ounces, 168 yards
(70 grams, 154 meters) per
    skein]: {4-5}{6-7-7}
    {8-9-10} skeins
Straight knitting needles,
    size 4 (3.5 mm) **or** size
    needed for gauge
16" (40.5 cm) Circular knitting
    needle, size 4 (3.5 mm)
Stitch holder
Marker
Tapestry needle

GAUGE: In Body pattern
(Sugar Cubes, page 27),
24 sts and 32 rows =
4" (10 cm)

Techniques used:
• K2 tog (*Fig. 1, page 139*)
• SSK (*Figs. 2a-c, page 140*)

BACK
RIBBING

With straight needles, cast on {98-114}{122-138-146} {162-170-186} sts.

Row 1: K2, (P2, K2) across.

Row 2 (Right side): P2, (K2, P2) across.

Repeat Rows 1 and 2 until Ribbing measures approximately 2" (5 cm) from cast on edge, ending by working a **wrong** side row.

BODY

Row 1 (Right side): Knit across.

Row 2: Purl across.

Row 3: K2, (P2, K6) across.

Row 4: (P6, K2) across to last 2 sts, P2.

Rows 5 and 6: Repeat Rows 1 and 2.

Row 7: (K6, P2) across to last 2 sts, K2.

Instructions continued on page 72.

Row 8: P2, (K2, P6) across.

Repeat Rows 1-8 for pattern until piece measures approximately 13½" (34.5 cm) from cast on edge, ending by working a **wrong** side row.

ARMHOLE SHAPING
Maintain established pattern throughout.

Rows 1 and 2: Bind off {5-8}{8-10-12}{16-18-22} sts, work across: {88-98}{106-118-122}{130-134-142} sts.

Row 3 (Decrease row): K1, SSK, work across to last 3 sts, K2 tog, K1: {86-96}{104-116-120}{128-132-140} sts.

Row 4: Work across.

Repeat Rows 3 and 4, {4-7}{7-10-12}{14-16-18} times: {78-82}{90-96-96}{100-100-104} sts.

Work even until Armholes measure approximately {6½-7}{7½-8-8½}{9-9½-10}"/{16.5-18}{19-20.5-21.5}{23-24-25.5} cm, ending by working a **wrong** side row.

SHOULDER SHAPING
Rows 1 and 2: Bind off {6-6}{7-8-8}{8-8-9} sts, work across: {66-70}{76-80-80}{84-84-86} sts.

Rows 3 and 4: Bind off {6-7}{7-8-8}{9-9-9} sts, work across: {54-56}{62-64-64}{66-66-68} sts.

Rows 5 and 6: Bind off {6-7}{8-8-8}{9-9-10} sts, work across: {42-42}{46-48-48}{48-48-48} sts.

Slip remaining sts onto st holder.

FRONT
Work same as Back until Armholes measure approximately {3½-4}{4½-4½-5}{5½-5½-6}"/{9-10}{11.5-11.5-12.5}{14-14-15} cm, ending by working a **wrong** side row: {78-82}{90-96-96}{100-100-104} sts.

NECK SHAPING
Both sides of Neck are worked at the same time, using separate yarn for **each** side.

Row 1: Work across {27-29}{31-34-34}{36-36-38} sts; with second yarn, bind off next {24-24}{28-28-28}{28-28-28} sts, work across: {27-29}{31-34-34}{36-36-38} sts **each** side.

Row 2: Work across; with second yarn, work across.

Row 3 (Decrease row): Work across to within 3 sts of Neck edge, K2 tog, K1; with second yarn, K1, SSK, work across: {26-28}{30-33-33}{35-35-37} sts **each** side.

Repeat Rows 2 and 3, {8-8}{8-9-9}{9-9-9} times: {18-20}{22-24-24}{26-26-28} sts **each** side.

Work even until Front measures same as Back to shoulders, ending by working a **wrong** side row.

SHOULDER SHAPING
Rows 1 and 2: Bind off {6-6}{7-8-8}{8-8-9} sts, work across; with second yarn, work across: {12-14}{15-16-16}{18-18-19} sts **each** side.

Rows 3 and 4: Bind off {6-7}{7-8-8}{9-9-9} sts, work across; with second yarn, work across: {6-7}{8-8-8}{9-9-10} sts **each** side.

Row 5: Bind off remaining sts on first side; with second yarn, work across.

Bind off remaining sts.

FINISHING
Sew shoulder seams. Weave side seams (*Fig. 8, page 141*).

NECK RIBBING
With **right** side facing and using circular needle, slip {42-42}{46-48-48}{48-48-48} sts from Back st holder onto circular knitting needle and knit across; pick up {23-23}{23-26-26}{26-30-30} sts evenly spaced along left Neck edge (*Figs. 7a & b, page 141*); pick up {24-24}{28-28-28}{28-28-28} sts across Front Neck edge; pick up {23-23}{23-26-26}{26-30-30} sts evenly spaced along right Neck edge; place marker to mark the beginning of the rnd (*see Markers, page 139*): {112-112}{120-128-128}{128-136-136} sts.

Rnds 1-5: (K2, P2) around.

Bind off all sts **loosely** in ribbing.

ARMHOLE RIBBING
With **right** side facing, using circular needles and beginning at side seam, pick up {92-100}{108-116-120}{128-136-140} sts evenly spaced around armhole edge; place marker to mark the beginning of the rnd.

Rnds 1-5: (K2, P2) around.

Bind off all sts in ribbing.

Repeat for second Armhole.

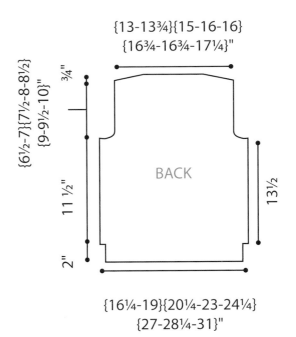

{13-13¾}{15-16-16}
{16¾-16¾-17¼}"

{6½-7}{7½-8-8½}
{9-9½-10}"

¾"

11 ½"

BACK

13½

2"

{16¼-19}{20¼-23-24¼}
{27-28¼-31}"

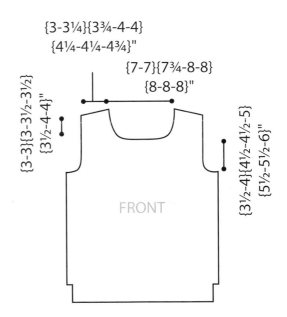

{3-3¼}{3¾-4-4}
{4¼-4¼-4¾}"

{7-7}{7¾-8-8}
{8-8-8}"

{3-3}{3-3½-3½}
{3½-4-4}"

{3½-4}{4½-4½-5}
{5½-5½-6}"

FRONT

Note: Shell includes two edge stitches.

WAVY RIB SWEATER

Easy stitch pattern mimics cables in this cropped, three-quarter sleeves sweater.

▰▰▱▱ **EASY**

Size	Finished Chest Measurement	
Extra Small	32¾"	(83 cm)
Small	37"	(94 cm)
Medium	41½"	(105.5 cm)
Large	46"	(117 cm)
Extra Large	50"	(127 cm)
2X-Large	54½"	(138.5 cm)
3X-Large	59"	(150 cm)
4X-Large	63¼"	(160.5 cm)

Size Note: Instructions are written with sizes Extra Small and Small in first set of braces { }, sizes Medium, Large, and Extra Large in the second set of braces, and sizes 2X-Large, 3X-Large, and 4X-Large in the third set of braces. Instructions will be easier to read if you circle all the numbers pertaining to your size. If only one number is given, it applies to all sizes.

MATERIALS

LIGHT 3

Light Weight Yarn
[1.75 ounces, 125 yards
(50 grams, 114 meters) per ball]:
{10-11}{13-15-16}
{18-20-22} balls
Straight knitting needles,
    sizes 6 (4 mm) **and**
    7 (4.5 mm) **or** sizes needed
    for gauge
16" (40.5 cm) Circular knitting
    needle, size 6 (4 mm)
Stitch holder
Marker
Tapestry needle

GAUGE: With larger size needles,
    in Body pattern
    [Wavy Rib (unstretched),
    page 34],
    22 sts and 26 rows =
    4" (10 cm)

Techniques used:
- K2 tog (*Fig. 1, page 139*)
- SSK (*Figs. 2a-c, page 140*)
- Knit increase (*Figs. 4a & b, page 140*)

BACK
RIBBING

With smaller size straight needles, cast on {92-104}{116-128-140} {152-164-176} sts.

Row 1: K2, (P4, K2) across.

Row 2: P2, (K4, P2) across.

Repeat Rows 1 and 2 until Ribbing measures approximately 3" (7.5 cm) from cast on edge, ending by working Row 1.

Instructions continued on page 76.

BODY

Change to larger size needles.

Row 1 (Right side): K3, P2, (K4, P2) across to last 3 sts, K3.

Row 2: P3, K2,(P3, K2) across to last 3 sts, P3.

Rows 3-6: Repeat Rows 1 and 2 twice.

Row 7: P2, (K4, P2) across.

Row 8: K2, (P4, K2) across.

Rows 9-12: Repeat Rows 7 and 8 twice.

Repeat Rows 1-12 for pattern until piece measures approximately {12½-12½}{12¾-12¾-12½} {12½-12¼-12}"/{32-32} {32.5-32.5-32}{32-31-30.5} cm from cast on edge, ending by working a **wrong** side row.

ARMHOLE SHAPING

Maintain established pattern throughout.

Rows 1 and 2: Bind off {5-6} {6-8-10}{12-16-18} sts, work across: {82-92}{104-112-120} {128-132-140} sts.

Row 3 (Decrease row): K1, SSK, work across to last 3 sts, K2 tog, K1: {80-90}{102-110-118} {126-130-138} sts.

Row 4: Work across.

Repeat Rows 3 and 4, {0-2}{4-6-9} {11-13-15} times (*see Zeros, page 139)*: {80-86}{94-98-100} {104-104-108} sts.

Work even until Armholes measure approximately {6½-7}{7½-8-8½} {9-9½-10}"/{16.5-18}{19-20.5-21.5} {23-24-25.5} cm, ending by working a **wrong** side row.

SHOULDER SHAPING

Rows 1 and 2: Bind off {6-6}{8-8-8} {8-8-9} sts, work across: {68-74} {78-82-84}{88-88-90} sts.

Rows 3 and 4: Bind off {6-6}{7-8-8} {9-9-9} sts, work across: {56-62} {64-66-68}{70-70-72} sts.

Rows 5 and 6: Bind off {6-6}{7-8-8} {9-9-10} sts, work across: {44-50} {50-50-52}{52-52-52} sts.

Slip remaining sts onto st holder.

FRONT

Work same as Back until Armholes measure approximately {3-3} {3½-4-4½}{5-5½-6}"/{7.5-7.5} {9-10-11.5}{12.5-14-15} cm, ending by working a **wrong** side row: {80-86}{94-98-100} {104-104-108} sts.

NECK SHAPING

Both sides of Neck are worked at the same time, using separate yarn for **each** side.

Row 1: Work across {32-34} {38-40-40}{42-42-44} sts; with second yarn, bind off next {16-18} {18-18-20}{20-20-20} sts, work across: {32-34}{38-40-40} {42-42-44} sts **each** side.

Rows 2-5: Work across; with second yarn, bind off 3 sts, work across: {26-28}{32-34-34} {36-36-38} sts **each** side.

Rows 6 and 7: Work across; with second yarn, bind off 2 sts, work across: {24-26}{30-32-32} {34-34-36} sts **each** side.

Row 8: Work across; with second yarn, work across.

Row 9: Work across to within 3 sts of Neck edge, K2 tog, K1; with second yarn, K1, SSK, work across: {23-25}{29-31-31}{33-33-35} sts **each** side.

Repeat Rows 8 and 9, {5-7}{7-7-7}{7-7-7} times: {18-18}{22-24-24}{26-26-28} sts **each** side.

Work even until Front measures same as Back to shoulders, ending by working a **wrong** side row.

SHOULDER SHAPING
Rows 1 and 2: Bind off {6-6}{8-8-8}{8-8-9} sts, work across: {12-12}{14-16-16}{18-18-19} sts **each** side.

Rows 3 and 4: Bind off {6-6}{7-8-8}{9-9-9} sts, work across: {6-6}{7-8-8}{9-9-10} sts **each** side.

Row 5: Bind off remaining sts on first side; with second yarn, work across.

Bind off remaining sts.

SLEEVE (Make 2)
RIBBING
With smaller size straight needles, cast on {50-56}{62-62-68}{68-74-80} sts.

Row 1: K2, (P4, K2) across.

Row 2: P2, (K4, P2) across.

Repeat Rows 1 and 2 until Ribbing measures approximately 3" (7.5 cm) from cast on edge, ending by working Row 1.

Instructions continued on page 78.

BODY
Change to larger size needles.

Work in pattern (Rows 1-12 of Back Body), increase one stitch at **each** edge, every {8-8}{8-6-6}{2-2-2} rows, {6-4}{6-9-9}{1-7-5} time(s); then increase every {0-10}{0-0-0} {4-4-4} rows, {0-2}{0-0-0} {14-11-13} times: {62-68}{74-80-86} {98-110-116} sts.

Work even until Sleeve measures approximately {11½-12} {12-12½-12½}{13-13-13½}"/ {29-30.5}{30.5-32-32} {33-33-34.5} cm from cast on edge, ending by working a **wrong** side row.

CAP SHAPING
Maintain established pattern throughout.

Rows 1 and 2: Bind off {5-6} {6-8-10}{12-16-18} sts, work across: {52-56}{62-64-66}{74-78-80} sts.

Row 3 (Decrease row)**:** K1, SSK, work across to last 3 sts, K2 tog, K1: {50-54}{60-62-64}{72-76-78} sts.

Row 4: Work across.

Repeat Rows 3 and 4, {9-10} {12-12-14}{14-15-17} times: {32-34} {36-38-36}{44-46-44} sts.

Next 2 Rows: Bind off {4-4}{4-5-4} {5-5-5} sts, work across: {24-26} {28-28-28}{34-36-34} sts.

Last 2 Rows: Bind off {4-4}{5-5-4} {6-6-5} sts, work across: {16-18} {18-18-20}{22-24-24} sts.

Bind off remaining sts.

FINISHING
Sew shoulder seams.

NECK RIBBING
With **right** side facing and using circular knitting needle, slip {44-50} {50-50-52}{52-52-52} sts from Back st holder onto circular knitting needle and knit across, pick up {21-22}{22-22-23}{23-23-23} sts evenly spaced along left Neck edge *(Figs. 7a & b, page 141)*, pick up {16-18}{18-18-20}{20-20-20} sts across Front Neck edge, pick up {21-22}{22-22-23}{23-23-23} sts evenly spaced along right Neck edge; place marker to mark the beginning of the rnd *(see Markers, page 139)*: {102-112}{112-112-118} {118-118-118} sts.

Rnds 1-6: (K1, P1) around.

Bind off all sts **loosely** in ribbing.

Sew Sleeves to sweater, placing center of last row on Sleeve Cap at shoulder seam and matching bound off stitches.

Weave side and underarm in one continuous seam *(Fig. 8, page 141)*.

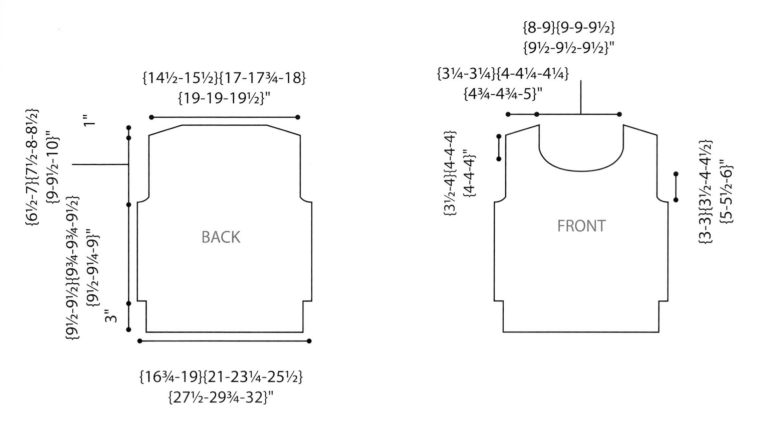

BACK

{14½-15½}{17-17¾-18}
{19-19-19½}"

1"

{6½-7}{7½-8-8½}
{9-9½-10}"

{9½-9½}{9¾-9¾-9½}
{9½-9¼-9}"

3"

{16¾-19}{21-23¼-25½}
{27½-29¾-32}"

FRONT

{8-9}{9-9-9½}
{9½-9½-9½}"

{3¼-3¼}{4-4¼-4¼}
{4¾-4¾-5}"

{3½-4}{4-4-4}
{4-4-4}"

{3-3}{3½-4-4½}
{5-5½-6}"

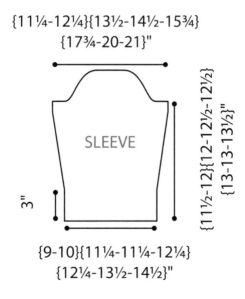

SLEEVE

{11¼-12¼}{13½-14½-15¾}
{17¾-20-21}"

{11½-12}{12-12½-12½}
{13-13-13½}"

3"

{9-10}{11¼-11¼-12¼}
{12¼-13½-14½}"

Note: Sweater includes two edge stitches.

BOY'S CREWNECK PULLOVER

Easy textured pattern in a large range of sizes!

EASY

Size	Finished Chest Measurement
4	26¼" (66.5 cm)
6	28½" (72.5 cm)
8	30½" (77.5 cm)
10	32¾" (83 cm)
12	35" (89 cm)
14	37" (94 cm)

Size Note: Instructions are written with sizes 4, 6, and 8 in the first set of braces { } and sizes 10, 12, and 14 in the second set of braces. Instructions will be easier to read if you circle all the numbers pertaining to your size. If only one number is given, it applies to all sizes.

MATERIALS
Light Weight Yarn
[3 ounces, 279 yards
(85 grams, 255 meters) per
   skein]: {2-3-3}{3-4-4} skeins
Straight knitting needles,
   sizes 5 (3.75 mm) **and**
   6 (4 mm) **or** sizes needed
   for gauge
16" (40.5 cm) Circular
   knitting needle,
   size 5 (3.75 mm)
Stitch holder
Marker
Tapestry needle

GAUGE: With larger size needles,
   in Body pattern
   (Swedish Block, page 26),
   22 sts and 32 rows =
   4" (10 cm)

Techniques used:
• K2 tog (*Fig. 1, page 139*)
• SSK (*Figs. 2a-c, page 140*)
• Knit increase (*Figs. 4a & b, page 140*)

BACK
RIBBING

With smaller size straight needles, cast on {73-79-85}{91-97-103} sts.

Row 1: P1, (K1, P1) across.

Row 2: K1, (P1, K1) across.

Repeat Rows 1 and 2 until Ribbing measures approximately 2" (5 cm), ending by working Row 2.

Last Row: Increase, (K1, P1) across: {74-80-86}{92-98-104} sts.

Instructions continued on page 82.

BODY
Change to larger size needles.

Row 1 (Right side)**:** (K2, P4) across to last 2 sts, K2.

Row 2: P2, (K4, P2) across.

Row 3: (P2, K4) across to last 2 sts, P2.

Row 4: K2, (P4, K2) across.

Rows 5-8: Repeat Rows 3 and 4 twice.

Repeat Rows 1-8 for pattern until piece measures approximately {9-10-11}{11½-12-13}"/{23-25.5-28} {29-30.5-33} cm from cast on edge, ending by working a **wrong** side row.

ARMHOLE SHAPING
Maintain established pattern throughout.

Rows 1 and 2: Bind off 6 sts, work across: {62-68-74}{80-86-92} sts.

Row 3 (Decrease row)**:** K1, SSK, work across to last 3 sts, K2 tog, K1: {60-66-72}{78-84-90} sts.

Row 4: Work across.

Repeat Rows 3 and 4, {3-5-6} {8-9-11} times: {54-56-60} {62-66-68} sts.

Work even until Armholes measure approximately {5-5½-6}{6½-7-7½}"/ {12.5-14-15}{16.5-18-19} cm, ending by working a **wrong** side row.

SHOULDER SHAPING
Rows 1 and 2: Bind off {4-4-5} {5-5-6} sts, work across: {46-48-50} {52-56-56} sts.

Rows 3 and 4: Bind off {5-5-5} {5-6-6} sts, work across: {36-38-40} {42-44-44} sts.

Rows 5 and 6: Bind off {5-5-5} {6-6-6} sts, work across: {26-28-30} {30-32-32} sts.

Slip remaining sts onto st holder.

FRONT
Work same as Back until Armholes measure approximately {3-3½-4} {4½-5-5½}"/{7.5-9-10} {11.5-12.5-14} cm, ending by working a **wrong** side row: {54-56-60}{62-66-68} sts.

NECK SHAPING
Both sides of Neck are worked at the same time using separate yarn for **each** side.

Row 1: Work across {18-18-19} {20-21-22} sts; with second yarn, bind off next {18-20-22} {22-24-24} sts, work across: {18-18-19}{20-21-22} sts **each** side.

Row 2: Work across; with second yarn, work across.

Row 3 (Decrease row)**:** Work across to within 3 sts of Neck edge, K2 tog, K1; with second yarn, K1, SSK, work across: {17-17-18}{19-20-21} sts **each** side.

Rows 4-9: Repeat Rows 2 and 3, 3 times: {14-14-15}{16-17-18} sts **each** side.

Work even until Front measures same as Back to shoulders, ending by working a **wrong** side row.

SHOULDER SHAPING
Rows 1 and 2: Bind off {4-4-5} {5-5-6} sts, work across: {10-10-10} {11-12-12} sts **each** side.

Rows 3 and 4: Bind off {5-5-5} {5-6-6} sts, work across: {5-5-5} {6-6-6} sts **each** side.

Row 5: Bind off remaining sts on first side; with second yarn, work across.

Bind off remaining sts.

SLEEVE (Make 2)
RIBBING
With smaller size straight needles, cast on {41-41-45}{45-49-49} sts.

Row 1: P1, (K1, P1) across.

Row 2: K1, (P1, K1) across.

Repeat Rows 1 and 2 until Ribbing measures approximately 2" (5 cm), ending by working Row 2.

Last Row: Increase, (K1, P1) across: {42-42-46}{46-50-50} sts.

BODY
Sizes 4, 6, 8, & 10 ONLY
Change to larger size needles.

Row 1 (Right side)**:** K{4-4-3}{3}, P4, (K2, P4) across to last {4-4-3}{3} sts, K{4-4-3}{3}.

Row 2: P{4-4-3}{3}, K4, (P2, K4) across to last {4-4-3}{3} sts, P{4-4-3}{3}.

Row 3: K{2-2-1}{1}, P2, (K4, P2) across to last {2-2-1}{1} st(s), K{2-2-1}{1}.

Row 4: P{2-2-1}{1}, K2, (P4, K2) across to last {2-2-1}{1} st(s), P{2-2-1}{1}.

Rows 5-8: Repeat Rows 3 and 4 twice.

Rows 9 and 10: Repeat Rows 1 and 2.

Row 11 (Increase row)**:** Increase, K{1-1-0}{0} *(see Zeros, page 139)*, P2, (K4, P2) across to last {2-2-1} {1} st(s), K{1-1-0}{0}, increase: {44-44-48}{48} sts.

Maintaining established pattern, continue to increase one stitch at **each** edge, every tenth row, {5-6-6} {7} times: {54-56-60}{62} sts.

Size 12 ONLY
Change to larger size needles.

Row 1 (Right side)**:** K1, P2, K2, (P4, K2) across to last 3 sts, P2, K1.

Row 2: P1, K2, P2, (K4, P2) across to last 3 sts, K2, P1.

Row 3: K3, P2, (K4, P2) across to last 3 sts, K3.

Row 4: P3, K2, (P4, K2) across to last 3 sts, P3.

Rows 5-8: Repeat Rows 3 and 4 twice.

Rows 9 and 10: Repeat Rows 1 and 2.

Row 11 (Increase row)**:** Increase, K2, P2, (K4, P2) across to last 3 sts, K2, increase: 52 sts.

Maintaining established pattern, continue to increase one stitch at **each** edge, every tenth row, 8 times: 68 sts.

Instructions continued on page 84.

Size 14 ONLY
Change to larger size needles.

Row 1 (Right side)**:** K1, P2, K2, (P4, K2) across to last 3 sts, P2, K1.

Row 2: P1, K2, P2, (K4, P2) across to last 3 sts, K2, P1.

Row 3: K3, P2, (K4, P2) across to last 3 sts, K3.

Row 4: P3, K2, (P4, K2) across to last 3 sts, P3.

Rows 5-8: Repeat Rows 3 and 4 twice.

Row 9 (Increase row)**:** Increase, P2, K2, (P4, K2) across to last 3 sts, P2, increase: 52 sts.

Maintaining established pattern, continue to increase one stitch at **each** edge, every eighth row once; then increase every tenth row, 9 times: 72 sts.

All SIZES
Work even until Sleeve measures approximately {10½-11½-12½} {13½-15-16}"/{26.5-29-32} {34.5-38-40.5} cm from cast on edge, ending by working a **wrong** side row.

CAP SHAPING
Maintain established pattern throughout.

Rows 1 and 2: Bind off 6 sts, work across: {42-44-48}{50-56-60} sts.

Row 3 (Decrease row)**:** K1, SSK, work across to last 3 sts, K2 tog, K1: {40-42-46}{48-54-58} sts.

Row 4: Work across.

Repeat Rows 3 and 4, {14-15-16} {17-19-21} times: {12-12-14} {14-16-16} sts.

Bind off remaining sts.

FINISHING
Sew shoulder seams.

NECK RIBBING
With **right** side facing and using circular needle, and beginning at right shoulder, slip {26-28-30} {30-32-32} sts from Back st holder onto circular needle and knit across, pick up 11 sts evenly spaced along left front Neck edge *(Figs. 7a & b, page 141)*, pick up {18-20-22} {22-24-24} sts across Front edge, pick up 11 sts evenly spaced along right front Neck edge, place marker to mark the beginning of the rnd *(see Markers, page 139)*: {66-70-74} {74-78-78} sts.

Rnds 1-5: (K1, P1) around.

Bind off all sts **loosely** in ribbing.

Sew Sleeves to sweater, placing center of last row on Sleeve Cap at shoulder seam and matching bound off stitches.

Weave side and underarm in one continuous seam *(Fig. 8, page 141)*.

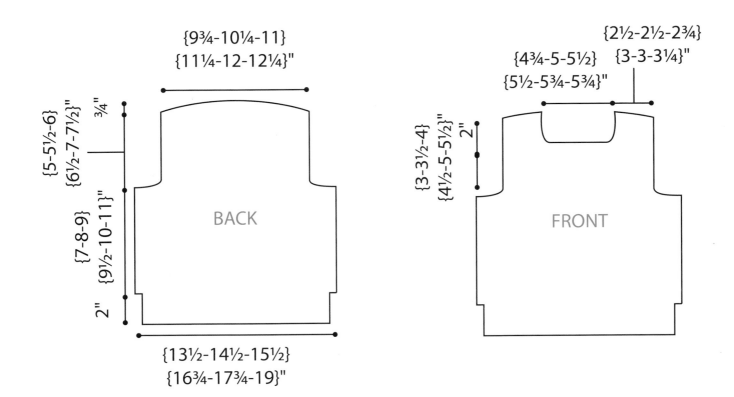

BACK

{9¾-10¼-11}
{11¼-12-12¼}"

{5-5½-6}
{6½-7-7½}"

¾"

{7-8-9}
{9½-10-11}"

2"

{13½-14½-15½}
{16¾-17¾-19}"

FRONT

{2½-2½-2¾}
{3-3-3¼}"

{4¾-5-5½}
{5½-5¾-5¾}"

{3-3½-4}
{4½-5-5½}"

2"

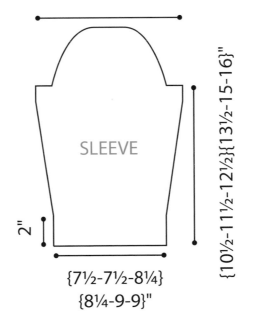

SLEEVE

{9¾-10¼-11}{11¼-12¼-13}"

{10½-11½-12½}{13½-15-16}"

2"

{7½-7½-8¼}
{8¼-9-9}"

Note: Pullover includes two edge stitches.

MEN'S BASKET WEAVE PULLOVER

Classic styling with a sporty dash of color!
A wide range of sizes makes this fun-to-stitch piece a sure fit.

◖◼◻◻◻ EASY

Size	Finished Chest Measurement	
Small	39½"	(100.5 cm)
Medium	42½"	(108 cm)
Large	45¾"	(116 cm)
Extra Large	48¾"	(124 cm)
2X-Large	51¾"	(131.5 cm)
3X-Large	54¾"	(139 cm)
4X-Large	58"	(147.5 cm)

Size Note: Instructions are written for size Small, with sizes Medium, Large, and Extra Large in the first set of braces { } and sizes 2X-Large, 3X-Large, and 4X-Large in the second set of braces. Instructions will be easier to read if you circle all the numbers pertaining to your size. If only one number is given, it applies to all sizes.

MATERIALS

Medium Weight Yarn
[3 ounces, 197 yards
(85 grams, 180 meters) per ball]:
  Grey - 8{9-10-11}
  {12-13-14} balls
  Red - one ball
Straight knitting needles,
  sizes 6 (4 mm) **and** 7 (4.5 mm)
  or sizes needed for gauge
16" (40.5 cm) Circular knitting
  needle, size 6 (4 mm)
Stitch holder
Marker
Yarn needle

GAUGE: With larger size needles,
In Body pattern
(Basket Weave, page 23),
21 sts and 34 rows =
4" (10 cm)

Techniques used:
- K2 tog (*Fig. 1, page 139*)
- SSK (*Figs. 2a-c, page 140*)
- Knit increase (*Figs. 4a & b, page 140*)

BACK
RIBBING

With smaller size straight needles and Red, cast on 106{114-122-130} {138-146-154} sts.

Row 1: P2, (K2, P2) across.

Cut Red.

Row 2: With Grey, K2, (P2, K2) across.

Row 3: P2, (K2, P2) across.

Row 4: K2, (P2, K2) across.

Repeat Rows 3 and 4 until Ribbing measures approximately 2½" (6.5 cm) from cast on edge, ending by working Row 3.

BODY

Change to larger size needles.

Row 1 (Right side)**:** K2, (P6, K2) across.

Row 2: P2, (K6, P2) across.

Row 3: Knit across.

Row 4: K4, (P2, K4) across.

Row 5: P4, (K2, P4) across.

Row 6: Purl across.

Repeat Rows 1-6 for pattern until piece measures approximately 16{16¼-16¼-16¼}{16¾-17¼-17¾}"/ 40.5{41.5-41.5-41.5}{42.5-44-45} cm from cast on edge, ending by working a **wrong** side row.

ARMHOLE SHAPING

Maintain established pattern throughout.

Rows 1 and 2: Bind off 6{6-7-8} {10-10-10} sts, work across: 94{102-108-114}{118-126-134} sts.

Row 3 (Decrease row)**:** K1, SSK, work across to last 3 sts, K2 tog, K1: 92{100-106-112}{116-124-132} sts.

Row 4: Work across.

Repeat Rows 3 and 4, 4{6-7-8} {8-10-12} times: 84{88-92-96} {100-104-108} sts.

Work even until Armholes measure approximately 9{9½-10-10¼} {10½-11-11½}"/23{24-25.5-26} {26.5-28-29} cm, ending by working a **wrong** side row.

Instructions continued on page 88.

SHOULDER SHAPING

Rows 1 and 2: Bind off 8{8-8-10}{10-10-10} sts, work across: 68{72-76-76}{80-84-88} sts.

Rows 3-6: Bind off 9{10-10-10}{10-11-12} sts, work across: 32{32-36-36}{40-40-40} sts.

Slip remaining sts onto st holder.

FRONT

Work same as Back until Armholes measure approximately 6½{7-7½-7¾}{8-8½-9}"/16.5{18-19-19.5}{20.5-21.5-23} cm, ending by working a **wrong** side row: 84{88-92-96}{100-104-108} sts.

NECK SHAPING

Both sides of Neck are worked at the same time, using separate yarn for **each** side.

Row 1: Work across 32{34-34-36}{36-38-40} sts; with second yarn, bind off next 20{20-24-24}{28-28-28} sts, work across: 32{34-34-36}{36-38-40} sts **each** side.

Row 2: Work across; with second yarn, work across.

Row 3 (Decrease row): Work across to within 3 sts of Neck edge, K2 tog, K1; with second yarn, K1, SSK, work across: 31{33-33-35}{35-37-39} sts **each** side.

Rows 4-13: Repeat Rows 2 and 3, 5 times: 26{28-28-30}{30-32-34} sts **each** side.

Work even until Front measures same as Back to shoulders, ending by working a **wrong** side row.

SHOULDER SHAPING

Rows 1 and 2: Bind off 8{8-8-10}{10-10-10} sts, work across: 18{20-20-20}{20-22-24} sts **each** side.

Rows 3 and 4: Bind off 9{10-10-10}{10-11-12} sts, work across: 9{10-10-10}{10-11-12} sts **each** side.

Row 5: Bind off remaining sts on first side; with second yarn, work across.

Bind off remaining sts.

SLEEVE (Make 2)
RIBBING

With smaller size straight needles and Red, cast on 50{50-58-58}{58-66-66} sts.

Row 1: P2, (K2, P2) across.

Cut Red.

Row 2: With Grey, K2, (P2, K2) across.

Row 3: P2, (K2, P2) across.

Row 4: K2, (P2, K2) across.

Repeat Rows 3 and 4 until Ribbing measures approximately 3" (7.5 cm) from cast on edge, ending by working Row 3.

BODY

Change to larger size needles.

Row 1 (Right side): K2, (P6, K2) across.

Row 2: P2, (K6, P2) across.

Row 3: Knit across.

Row 4: K4, (P2, K4) across.

Row 5: P4, (K2, P4) across.

Row 6: Purl across.

Row 7 (Increase row): Increase, K1, P6, (K2, P6) across to last 2 sts, K1, increase: 52{52-60-60}{60-68-68} sts.

Maintaining established pattern, continue increasing one stitch at **each** edge, every fourth row, 1{0-0-0}{0-0-4} time(s) *(see Zeros, page 139)*; then increase every sixth row, 18{18-12-15}{13-17-19} times; then increase every eighth row, 0{1-6-5}{7-4-0} time(s): 90{90-96-100}{100-110-114} sts.

Work even until Sleeve measures approximately 18{18½-19-20}{20½-20½-20½}"/45.5{47-48.5-51}{52-52-52} cm from cast on edge, ending by working a **wrong** side row.

CAP SHAPING

Maintain established pattern throughout.

Rows 1 and 2: Bind off 6{6-7-8}{10-10-10} sts; work across: 78{78-82-84}{80-90-94} sts.

Row 3 (Decrease row): K1, SSK, work across to last 3 sts, K2 tog, K1: 76{76-80-82}{78-88-92} sts.

Row 4: Work across.

Repeat Rows 3 and 4, 23{23-25-25}{23-27-29} times: 30{30-30-32}{32-34-34} sts.

Next 2 Rows: Bind off 3{3-2-3} {2-2-2} sts, work across: 24{24-26-26}{28-30-30} sts.

Last 2 Rows: Bind off 3{3-3-3} {3-3-2} sts, work across: 18{18-20-20}{22-24-26} sts.

Bind off remaining sts.

FINISHING

Sew shoulder seams.

NECK RIBBING

With **right** side facing and using circular needle, and beginning at right shoulder, slip 32{32-36-36} {40-40-40} sts from Back st holder onto circular needle and knit across, pick up 20 sts evenly spaced along left Neck edge *(Figs. 7a & b, page 141)*, pick up 20{20-24-24} {28-28-28} sts across Front Neck edge, pick up 20 sts evenly spaced along right Neck edge; place marker to mark the beginning of the rnd *(see Markers, page 139)*: 92{92-100-100}{108-108-108} sts.

Rnds 1-6: (K2, P2) around.

Cut Grey.

Rnd 7: With Red, (K2, P2) around.

Bind off all sts **loosely** in ribbing.

Sew Sleeves to sweater, placing center of last row on Sleeve Cap at shoulder seam and matching bound off stitches.

Weave side and underarm in one continuous seam *(Fig. 8, page 141)*.

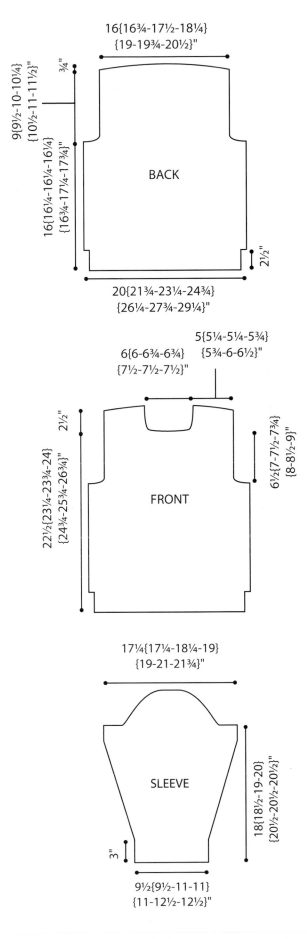

Note: Pullover includes two edge stitches.

HIS ZIGZAG PULLOVER

Six different sizes make this sweater a perfect fit for the man on your gift list!

◼◼◻◻ EASY

Size	Finished Chest Measurement	
Small	39½"	(100.5 cm)
Medium	42"	(106.5 cm)
Large	47"	(119.5 cm)
Extra Large	49¾"	(126.5 cm)
2X-Large	54¾"	(139 cm)
3X-Large	57¼"	(145.5 cm)

Size Note: Instructions are written with sizes Small, Medium, and Large in the first set of braces { } and sizes Extra Large, 2X-Large, and 3X-Large in the second set of braces. Instructions will be easier to read if you circle all the numbers pertaining to your size. If only one number is given, it applies to all sizes.

MATERIALS

MEDIUM 4

Medium Weight Yarn [1.76 ounces, 87 yards (50 grams, 80 meters) per skein]: {17-18-21}{23-25-27} skeins
Straight knitting needles, sizes 5 (3.75 mm) **and** 7 (4.5 mm) **or** sizes needed for gauge
16" (40.5 cm) Circular knitting needle, size 5 (3.75 mm)
Stitch holder
Marker
Yarn needle

GAUGE: With larger size needles, in Body pattern (Garter Zigzag, page 33), 19 sts and 32 rows = 4" (10 cm)

Techniques used:
- K2 tog *(Fig. 1, page 139)*
- SSK *(Figs. 2a-c, page 140)*
- Knit increase *(Figs. 4a & b, page 140)*

BACK
RIBBING

With smaller size straight needles, cast on {96-102-114}{120-132-138} sts.

Row 1: (K1, P1) across.

Row 2 (Right side): (K3, P3) across.

Repeat Rows 1 and 2 until Ribbing measures approximately 2½" (6.5 cm) from cast on edge, ending by working Row 1.

BODY
Change to larger needles.

Row 1 AND ALL RIGHT SIDE ROWS: Knit across.

Row 2: (K3, P3) across.

Row 4: K2, P3, (K3, P3) across to last st, K1.

Instructions continued on page 92.

Row 6: K1, P3, (K3, P3) across to last 2 sts, K2.

Row 8: (P3, K3) across.

Row 10: K1, P3, (K3, P3) across to last 2 sts, K2.

Row 12: K2, P3, (K3, P3) across to last st, K1.

Repeat Rows 1-12 for pattern until piece measures approximately 16¼" (41.5 cm) from cast on edge, ending by working a **wrong** side row.

ARMHOLE SHAPING

Maintain established pattern throughout.

Rows 1 and 2: Bind off {6-6-7}{8-10-12} sts, work across: {84-90-100}{104-112-114} sts.

Row 3 (Decrease row)**:** K1, SSK, work across to last 3 sts, K2 tog, K1: {82-88-98}{102-110-112} sts.

Row 4: Work across.

Repeat Rows 3 and 4, {5-6-9}{9-12-12} times: {72-76-80}{84-86-88} sts.

Work even until Armholes measure approximately {9-9½-10}{10½-11-11½}"/{23-24-25.5}{26.5-28-29} cm, ending by working a **wrong** side row.

SHOULDER SHAPING

Rows 1 and 2: Bind off {6-7-7}{8-8-8} sts, work across: {60-62-66}{68-70-72} sts.

Rows 3 and 4: Bind off {7-7-7}{8-8-8} sts, work across: {46-48-52}{52-54-56} sts.

Rows 5 and 6: Bind off {7-7-8}{8-8-8} sts, work across: {32-34-36}{36-38-40} sts.

Slip remaining sts onto st holder.

FRONT

Work same as Back until Armholes measure approximately {6-6½-7}{7½-8-8½}"/{15-16.5-18}{19-20.5-21.5} cm, ending by working a **wrong** side row: {72-76-80}{84-86-88} sts.

NECK SHAPING

Both sides of Neck are worked at the same time, using separate yarn for **each** side.

Row 1: Work across {28-29-30}{32-32-32} sts; with second yarn, bind off next {16-18-20}{20-22-24} sts, work across: {28-29-30}{32-32-32} sts **each** side.

Row 2: Work across; with second yarn, work across.

Row 3 (Decrease row)**:** Work across to within 3 sts of Neck edge, K2 tog, K1; with second yarn, K1, SSK, work across: {27-28-29}{31-31-31} sts **each** side.

Rows 4-17: Repeat Rows 2 and 3, 7 times: {20-21-22}{24-24-24} sts **each** side.

Work even until Front measures same as Back to shoulder, ending by working a **wrong** side row.

SHOULDER SHAPING

Rows 1 and 2: Bind off {6-7-7}{8-8-8} sts, work across: {14-14-15}{16-16-16} sts **each** side.

Rows 3 and 4: Bind off {7-7-7}{8-8-8} sts, work across: {7-7-8}{8-8-8} sts **each** side.

Row 5: Bind off remaining sts on first side; with second yarn, work across.

Bind off remaining sts.

SLEEVE (Make 2)
RIBBING

With smaller size straight needles, cast on {48-48-54}{54-60-60} sts.

Row 1: (K1, P1) across.

Row 2 (Right side)**:** (K3, P3) across.

Repeat Rows 1 and 2 until Ribbing measures approximately 3" (7.5 cm) from cast on edge, ending by working Row 1.

BODY

Change to larger size needles.

Working in pattern (Rows 1-12 of Back Body), increase one stitch at **each** edge, every fourth row, {0-0-0}{2-0-6} times (*see Zeros, page 139*); then increase every sixth row, {4-10-6}{20-18-18} times; then increase every eighth row, {11-7-11}{0-3-0} times: {78-82-88}{98-102-108} sts.

Work even until Sleeve measures approximately {18-18½-19½}{20-20½-20½}"/{45.5-47-49.5}{51-52-52} cm from cast on edge, ending by working a **wrong** side row.

CAP SHAPING

Maintain established pattern throughout.

Rows 1 and 2: Bind off {6-6-7} {8-10-12} sts, work across: {66-70-74}{82-82-84} sts.

Row 3: K1, SSK, work across to last 3 sts, K2 tog, K1: {64-68-72} {80-80-82} sts.

Row 4: Work across.

Repeat Rows 3 and 4, {21-21-21} {23-25-27} times: {22-26-30} {34-30-28} sts.

Next 2 Rows: Bind off {2-3-3} {4-3-2} sts, work across: {18-20-24} {26-24-24} sts.

Next 2 Rows: Bind off {2-3-4} {4-3-2} sts, work across: {14-14-16} {18-18-20} sts.

Bind off remaining sts.

FINISHING

Sew shoulder seams.

NECK RIBBING

With **right** side facing and using circular needle, slip {32-34-36} {36-38-40} sts from Back st holder onto circular needle and knit across, pick up {21-22-20}{23-21-22} sts evenly spaced along left Neck edge *(Figs. 7a & b, page 141)*, pick up {16-18-20}{20-22-24} sts across Front Neck edge, pick up {21-22-20} {23-21-22} sts evenly spaced along right Neck edge; place marker to mark the beginning of the rnd *(see Markers, page 139)*: {90-96-96} {102-102-108} sts.

Rnd 1: (K3, P3) around.

Rnd 2: (K1, P1) around.

Repeat Rnds 1 and 2 until Ribbing measures approximately 1"(2.5 cm).

Bind off all sts **loosely** in ribbing.

Sew Sleeves to sweater, placing center of last row on Sleeve Cap at shoulder seam and matching bound off stitches.

Weave side and underarm in one continuous seam *(Fig. 8, page 141)*.

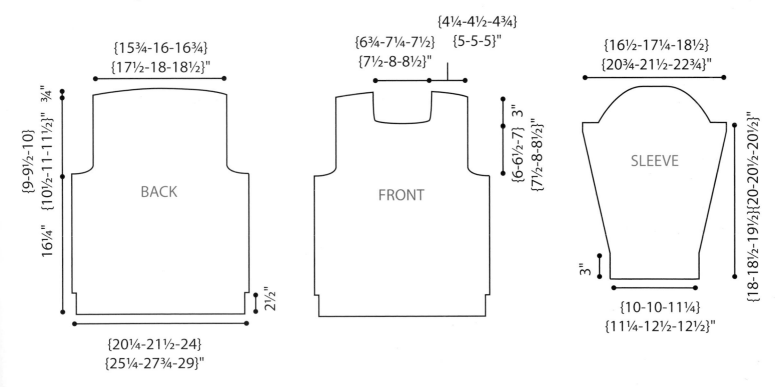

Note: Pullover includes two edge stitches.

HER ZIGZAG TUNIC

A simple stitch change creates a close-fitting bodice and flared "skirt" in this tunic-length charmer.

■■□□ EASY

Size	Finished Chest Measurement	
Extra Small	31¼"	(79.5 cm)
Small	35¼"	(89.5 cm)
Medium	39¼"	(99.5 cm)
Large	43¼"	(110 cm)
Extra Large	47¼"	(120 cm)
2X-Large	51¼"	(130 cm)
3X-Large	55¼"	(140.5 cm)

Size Note: Instructions are written for size Extra Small, with sizes Small, Medium, and Large in the first set of braces { } and sizes Extra Large, 2X-Large, and 3X-Large in the second set of braces. Instructions will be easier to read if you circle all the numbers pertaining to your size. If only one number is given, it applies to all sizes.

MATERIALS

MEDIUM 4

Medium Weight Yarn [1.75 ounces, 87 yards (50 grams, 80 meters) per skein]: 15{16-18-20}{22-25-27} skeins
Straight knitting needles, sizes 5 (3.75 mm) **and** 7 (4.5 mm) **or** sizes needed for gauge
16" (40.5 cm) Circular knitting needle, size 5 (3.75 mm)
Stitch holder
Marker
Yarn needle

GAUGE: With larger size needles, in Body pattern (Garter Zigzag, page 33), 19 sts and 32 rows = 4" (10 cm); In Bodice pattern (Twin Rib, page 13), 24 sts and 26 rows = 4" (10 cm)

Techniques used:
- K2 tog (*Fig. 1, page 139*)
- SSK (*Figs. 2a-c, page 140*)
- Knit increase (*Figs. 4a & b, page 140*)

BACK
BAND
Using smaller size needles, cast on 96{108-120-132} {144-156-168} sts.

Rows 1-5: Knit across (Garter Stitch).

BODY
Change to larger size knitting needles.

Row 1 AND ALL RIGHT SIDE ROWS: Knit across.

Row 2: (K3, P3) across.

Instructions continued on page 96.

Instructions continued on page 96.

Row 4: K2, P3, (K3, P3) across to last st, K1.

Row 6: K1, P3, (K3, P3) across to last 2 sts, K2.

Row 8: (P3, K3) across.

Row 10: K1, P3, (K3, P3) across to last 2 sts, K2.

Row 12: K2, P3, (K3, P3) across to last st, K1.

Repeat Rows 1-12 for pattern until piece measures approximately 18¼" (46.5 cm) from cast on edge, ending by working a **wrong** side row.

BODICE
Row 1: (K3, P3) across.

Row 2: (K1, P1) across.

Repeat Rows 1 and 2 until piece measures approximately 22¼" (56.5 cm) from cast on edge, ending by working Row 2.

ARMHOLE SHAPING
Maintain established pattern throughout.

Rows 1 and 2: Bind off 5{5-6-6} {8-10-14} sts, work across: 86{98-108-120}{128-136-140} sts.

Row 3 (Decrease row)**:** K2, SSK, work across to last 4 sts, K2 tog, K2: 84{96-106-118}{126-134-138} sts.

Row 4: Work across.

Repeat Rows 3 and 4, 0{4-5-8} {10-13-15} times *(see Zeros, page 139)*: 84{88-96-102} {106-108-108} sts.

Work even until Armholes measure approximately 6½{7-7½-8} {8½-9-9½}"/16.5{18-19-20.5} {21.5-23-24} cm, ending by working a **wrong** side row.

SHOULDER SHAPING
Rows 1 and 2: Bind off 7{7-9-9} {9-10-10} sts, work across: 70{74-78-84}{88-88-88} sts.

Rows 3-6: Bind off 7{8-9-9} {10-10-10} sts, work across: 42{42-42-48}{48-48-48} sts.

Slip remaining sts onto st holder.

FRONT
Work same as Back until Armholes measure approximately 3½{4-4½-5} {5½-6-6½}"/9{10-11.5-12.5} {14-15-16.5} cm, ending by working a **wrong** side row: 84{88-96-102} {106-108-108} sts.

NECK SHAPING
Both sides of Neck are worked at the same time, using separate yarn for **each** side.

Row 1: Work across 34{36-40-42} {44-45-45} sts; with second yarn, bind off next 16{16-16-18} {18-18-18} sts, work across: 34{36-40-42}{44-45-45} sts **each** side.

Row 2: Work across; with second yarn, work across.

Rows 3 and 4: Work across; with second yarn, bind off 3 sts, work across: 31{33-37-39}{41-42-42} sts **each** side.

Rows 5-8: Work across; with second yarn, bind off 2{2-2-3} {3-3-3} sts, work across: 27{29-33-33}{35-36-36} sts **each** side.

Row 9: Work across; with second yarn, work across.

Row 10 (Decrease row)**:** Work across to within 3 sts of Neck edge, K2 tog, K1; with second yarn, K1, SSK, work across: 26{28-32-32}{34-35-35} sts **each** side.

Rows 11-20: Repeat Rows 9 and 10, 5 times: 21{23-27-27}{29-30-30} sts **each** side.

Work even until Front measures same as Back to shoulders, ending by working a **wrong** side row.

SHOULDER SHAPING

Rows 1 and 2: Bind off 7{7-9-9}{9-10-10} sts, work across: 14{16-18-18}{20-20-20} sts **each** side.

Rows 3 and 4: Bind off 7{8-9-9}{10-10-10} sts, work across: 7{8-9-9}{10-10-10} sts **each** side.

Row 5: Bind off remaining sts on first side; with second yarn, work across.

Bind off remaining sts.

SLEEVE (Make 2)
RIBBING

With larger size needles, cast on 54{54-54-60}{60-66-66} sts.

Row 1: (K3, P3) across.

Row 2: (K1, P1) across.

Repeat Rows 1 and 2 until Ribbing measures approximately 5" (12.5 cm) from cast on edge, ending by working Row 2.

BODY

Working in Back Body pattern (Rows 1-12), increase one stitch at **each** edge, every 28{22-14-18}{10-8-6} rows, 3{4-4-4}{8-5-8} times; then increase every 0{0-16-20}{12-10-8} rows, 0{0-2-1}{1-5-6} time(s): 60{62-66-70}{78-86-94} sts.

Work even until Sleeve measures approximately 16½{17-17-17½}{17½-18-18}"/42{43-43-44.5}{44.5-45.5-45.5} cm from cast on edge, ending by working a **wrong** side row.

CAP SHAPING

Maintain established pattern throughout.

Rows 1 and 2: Bind off 5{5-6-6}{8-10-14} sts, work across: 52{54-56-60}{64-68-68} sts.

Row 3 (Decrease row)**:** K2, SSK, work across to last 4 sts, K2tog, K2: 50{52-54-58}{62-66-66} sts

Row 4: Work across.

Repeat Rows 3 and 4, 10{12-14-14}{16-16-18} times: 30{28-26-30}{30-34-30} sts.

Last 4 Rows: Bind off 3{2-2-2}{2-3-2} sts, work across: 18{20-18-22}{22-22-22} sts.

Bind off remaining sts.

Instructions continued on page 98.

FINISHING

Sew shoulder seams.

NECK RIBBING

With **right** side facing and using circular knitting needle, slip 42{42-42-48}{48-48-48} sts from Back st holder onto circular knitting needle and knit across, pick up 25 sts evenly spaced along left Neck edge *(Figs. 7a & b, page 141)*, pick up 16{16-16-18}{18-18-18} across Front Neck edge, pick up 25 sts evenly spaced along right Neck edge; place marker to mark the beginning of the rnd *(see Markers, page 139)*: 108{108-108-116}{116-116-116} sts.

Rnds 1-6: (K2, P2) around.

Bind off all sts **loosely** in Ribbing.

Sew Sleeves to sweater, placing center of last row on Sleeve Cap at shoulder seam and matching bound off stitches.

Weave side and underarm in one continuous seam *(Fig. 8, page 141)*.

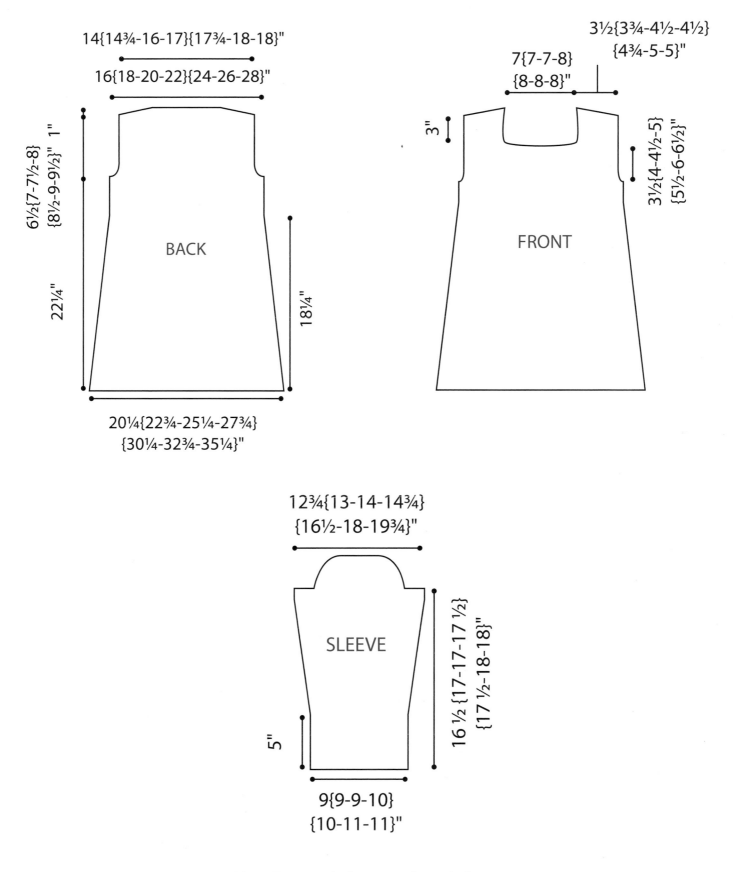

14{14¾-16-17}{17¾-18-18}"

16{18-20-22}{24-26-28}"

6½{7-7½-8}
{8½-9-9½}" 1"

BACK

22¼"

18¼"

20¼{22¾-25¼-27¾}
{30¼-32¾-35¼}"

3½{3¾-4½-4½}
{4¾-5-5}"

7{7-7-8}
{8-8-8}"

3"

FRONT

3½{4-4½-5}
{5½-6-6½}"

12¾{13-14-14¾}
{16½-18-19¾}"

SLEEVE

16 ½ {17-17-17 ½}
{17 ½-18-18}"

5"

9{9-9-10}
{10-11-11}"

Note: Tunic includes two edge stitches.

LADIES V-NECK CARDIGAN

A classic piece that will be welcome in any wardrobe.

▰▰▰▰▱ INTERMEDIATE

Size	Finished Chest Measurement	
Extra Small	33½"	(85 cm)
Small	37¾"	(96 cm)
Medium	42¼"	(107 cm)
Large	46½"	(118 cm)
Extra Large	51"	(129.5 cm)
2X-Large	55¼"	(140.5 cm)
3X-Large	59½"	(151 cm)

Size Note: Instructions are written for size Extra Small, with sizes Small, Medium, and Large in the first set of braces { } and sizes Extra Large, 2X-Large, and 3X-Large in the second set of braces. Instructions will be easier to read if you circle all the numbers pertaining to your size. If only one number is given, it applies to all sizes.

MATERIALS

MEDIUM 4

Medium Weight Yarn [3.5 ounces, 217 yards (100 grams, 198 meters) per hank]:
  6{6-7-8}{9-9-10} hanks
Straight knitting needles, sizes 5 (3.75 cm) **and** 6 (4 mm) **or** sizes needed for gauge 29" (73.5 mm)
Circular knitting needle, size 5 (3.75 mm)
Stitch holder
Yarn needle
Sewing needle and thread
1" (25 mm) Buttons - 6

GAUGE: With larger size needles, in Body pattern (Little Knot, page 27), 22 sts and 29 rows = 4" (10 cm)

Techniques used:
- K2 tog (*Fig. 1, page 139*)
- SSK (*Figs. 2a-c, page 140*)
- Knit increase (*Figs. 4a & b, page 140*)
- Adding New Stitches (*Figs. 6a & b, page 141*)

BACK
RIBBING

With smaller size straight needles, cast on 95{107-119-131}{143-155-167} sts.

Row 1: P1, (K1, P1) across.

Row 2: K1, (P1, K1) across.

Repeat Rows 1 and 2 until Ribbing measures approximately 2" (5 cm) from cast on edge, ending by working Row 1.

BODY

Change to larger size needles.

Row 1 (Right side)**:** K4, P1, K1, P1, (K3, P1, K1, P1) across to last 4 sts, K4.

Row 2: P4, K3, (P3, K3) across to last 4 sts, P4.

Instructions continued on page 102.

Row 3: K4, P1, K1, P1, (K3, P1, K1, P1) across to last 4 sts, K4.

Row 4: Purl across.

Row 5: (K1, P1) twice, K3, (P1, K1, P1, K3) across to last 4 sts, (P1, K1) twice.

Row 6: P1, K3, (P3, K3) across to last st, P1.

Row 7: (K1, P1) twice, K3, (P1, K1, P1, K3) across to last 4 sts, (P1, K1) twice.

Row 8: Purl across.

Repeat Rows 1-8 for pattern until Back measures approximately 15¼{15¼-15-14¾} {14½-14¼-13¾}"/38.5{38.5-38-37.5} {37-36-35} cm from cast on edge, ending by working a **wrong** side row.

ARMHOLE SHAPING
Maintain established pattern throughout.

Rows 1 and 2: Bind off 5{6-6-8} {10-10-10} sts, work across: 85{95-107-115}{123-135-147} sts.

Sizes Extra Large, 2X-Large, & 3X-Large ONLY
Next {2-4-6} Rows: Bind off 3 sts, work across: {117-123-129} sts.

ALL SIZES
Decrease Row: K1, SSK, work across to last 3 sts, K2 tog, K1: 83{93-105-113}{115-121-127} sts.

Next Row: Work across.

Repeat last 2 rows, 0{3-5-6}{7-9-12} times *(see Zeros, page 139)*: 83{87-95-101}{101-103-103} sts.

Work even until Armholes measure approximately 6½{7-7½-8} {8½-9-9½}"/16.5{18-19-20.5} {21.5-23-24} cm, ending by working a **wrong** side row.

SHOULDER SHAPING
Rows 1 and 2: Bind off 7{8-8-9} {9-9-9} sts, work across: 69{71-79-83}{83-85-85} sts.

Rows 3 and 4: Bind off 7{8-9-9} {9-10-10} sts, work across: 55{55-61-65}{65-65-65} sts.

Rows 5 and 6: Bind off 8{8-9-10} {10-10-10} sts, work across: 39{39-43-45}{45-45-45} sts.

Slip remaining sts onto st holder.

RIGHT FRONT
With smaller size straight needles, cast on 44{50-56-62}{68-74-80} sts.

Work in K1, P1 ribbing for 2" (5 cm).

BODY
Change to larger size needles.

Row 1 (Right side): K4, (P1, K1, P1, K3) across to last 4 sts, (P1, K1) twice.

Row 2: P1, K3, (P3, K3) across to last 4 sts, P4.

Row 3: K4, (P1, K1, P1, K3) across to last 4 sts, (P1, K1) twice.

Row 4: Purl across.

Row 5: (K1, P1) twice, (K3, P1, K1, P1) across to last 4 sts, K4.

Row 6: P4, K3, (P3, K3) across to last st, P1.

Row 7: (K1, P1) twice, (K3, P1, K1, P1) across to last 4 sts, K4.

Row 8: Purl across.

Repeat Rows 1-8 for pattern until Right Front measures approximately 13{13½-12¾-12¼} {12½-12¾-12¾}"/33{34.5-32.5-31} {32-32.5-32.5} cm from cast on edge, ending by working a **wrong** side row.

NECK & ARMHOLE SHAPING
Maintain established pattern throughout.

Row 1: K1, SSK, work across: 43{49-55-61}{67-73-79} sts.

Continue to decrease in same manner every fourth row, 15{15-17-18}{18-18-18} times AND AT THE SAME TIME, when piece measures same as Back to underarm, bind off 5{6-6-8} {10-10-10} sts at armhole edge; then bind off 3 sts at armhole edge, 0{0-0-0}{1-2-3} time(s); then decrease one st at armhole edge (one st in), every **right** side row, 1{4-6-7}{8-10-13} time(s): 22{24-26-28}{28-29-29} sts.

Work even until Right Front measures same as Back to shoulder, ending by working a **right** side row.

SHOULDER SHAPING
Row 1: Bind off 7{8-8-9}{9-9-9} sts, work across: 15{16-18-19} {19-20-20} sts.

Row 2: Work across.

Row 3: Bind off 7{8-9-9} {9-10-10} sts, work across: 8{8-9-10}{10-10-10} sts.

Row 4: Work across.

Bind off remaining sts.

LEFT FRONT
With smaller size straight needles, cast on 44{50-56-62} {68-74-80} sts.

Work in K1, P1 Ribbing for 2" (5 cm).

BODY
Change to larger size needles.

Row 1 (Right side)**:** (K1, P1) twice, (K3, P1, K1, P1) across to last 4 sts, K4.

Row 2: P4, K3, (P3, K3) across to last st, P1.

Row 3: (K1, P1) twice, (K3, P1, K1, P1) across to last 4 sts, K4.

Row 4: Purl across.

Row 5: K4, (P1, K1, P1, K3) across to last 4 sts, (P1, K1) twice.

Row 6: P1, K3, (P3, K3) across to last 4 sts, P4.

Row 7: K4, (P1, K1, P1, K3) across to last 4 sts, (P1, K1) twice.

Row 8: Purl across.

Repeat Rows 1-8 for pattern until Left Front measures same as Right Front to Neck Shaping, ending by working a **wrong** side row.

NECK & ARMHOLE SHAPING
Maintain established pattern throughout.

Row 1: Work across to last 3 sts, K2 tog, K1: 43{49-55-61} {67-73-79} sts.

Instructions continued on page 104.

Continue to decrease in same manner every fourth row, 15{15-17-18}{18-18-18} times AND AT THE SAME TIME when piece measures same as Back to underarm, bind off 5{6-6-8}{10-10-10} sts at armhole edge; then bind off 3 sts at armhole edge 0{0-0-0}{1-2-3} time(s); then decrease one st at armhole edge (one st in), every **right** side row, 1{4-6-7}{8-10-13} time(s): 22{24-26-28}{28-29-29} sts.

Work even until Left Front measures same as Back to shoulder, ending by working a **wrong** side row.

SHOULDER SHAPING
Row 1: Bind off 7{8-8-9}{9-9-9} sts, work across: 15{16-18-19}{19-20-20} sts.

Row 2: Work across.

Row 3: Bind off 7{8-9-9}{9-10-10} sts, work across: 8{8-9-10}{10-10-10} sts.

Row 4: Work across.

Bind off remaining sts.

SLEEVE (Make 2)
RIBBING
With smaller size straight needles, cast on 44{50-50-50}{56-56-62} sts.

Work in K1, P1 ribbing for 3" (7.5 cm).

BODY
Change to larger size needles.

Working in Right Front Body pattern (Rows 1-12), increase one stitch at **each** edge; every fourth row, 0{0-0-11}{14-15-18} times; then increase every sixth row, 3{1-13-9}{7-7-5} times; then increase every eighth row, 9{11-2-0}{0-0-0} times: 68{74-80-90}{98-100-108} sts.

Work even until Sleeve measures approximately 16½{17-17-17½}{17½-18-18}"/42{43-43-44.5}{44.5-45.5-45.5} cm from cast on edge, ending by working a **wrong** side row.

CAP SHAPING
Maintain established pattern throughout.

Rows 1 and 2: Bind off 5{6-6-8}{10-10-10} sts, work across: 58{62-68-74}{78-80-88} sts.

Row 3 (Decrease row)**:** K1, SSK, work across to last 3 sts, K2 tog, K1: 56{60-66-72}{76-78-86} sts.

Row 4: Work across.

Repeat Rows 3 and 4, 10{12-12-14}{14-16-17} times: 36{36-42-44}{48-46-52} sts.

Next 2 Rows: Bind off 5{5-6-6}{7-6-7} sts, work across: 26{26-30-32}{34-34-38} sts.

Next 2 Rows: Bind off 5{5-6-6}{6-6-7} sts, work across: 16{16-18-20}{22-22-24} sts.

Bind off remaining sts in pattern.

FINISHING
Sew shoulder seams.

BAND
With **right** side facing, using circular needle and beginning at lower Right Front, pick up 86{92-84-82}{82-84-84} sts across to beginning of Right Neck Shaping (*Figs. 7a & b, page 141*), pick up 64{62-70-74}{74-74-74} sts evenly spaced along Neck Shaping; slip 39{39-43-45}{45-45-45} sts from Back st holder onto opposite end of circular needle and knit across; pick up 64{62-70-74}{74-74-74} sts evenly spaced along Left Neck Shaping; pick up 86{92-84-82}{82-84-84} sts across Left Front edge: 339{347-351-351}{357-367-367} sts.

Row 1: P1, (K1, P1) across.

Row 2 (Right side)**:** K1, (P1, K1) across.

Row 3: P1, (K1, P1) across.

Row 4 (Buttonhole row begun)**:** K1, (P1, K1) 2{2-3-2}{2-3-3} times, bind off next 3 sts, ★ P1, (K1, P1) 5{6-5-5}{5-5-5} times, bind off next 3 sts; repeat from ★ 4 times **more**, work in established pattern across.

Row 5 (Buttonhole row completed)**:** ★ Work in established pattern across to bound off sts, **turn**; add on 3 sts, **turn**; repeat from ★ 5 times **more**, work in established pattern across.

Rows 6-9: Repeat Rows 2 and 3 twice.

Bind off all sts in pattern.

Sew Sleeves to sweater, placing center of last row on Sleeve Cap at shoulder seam and matching bound off stitches.

Weave side and underarm in one continuous seam *(Fig. 8, page 141)*.

Sew buttons to left front Band opposite buttonholes.

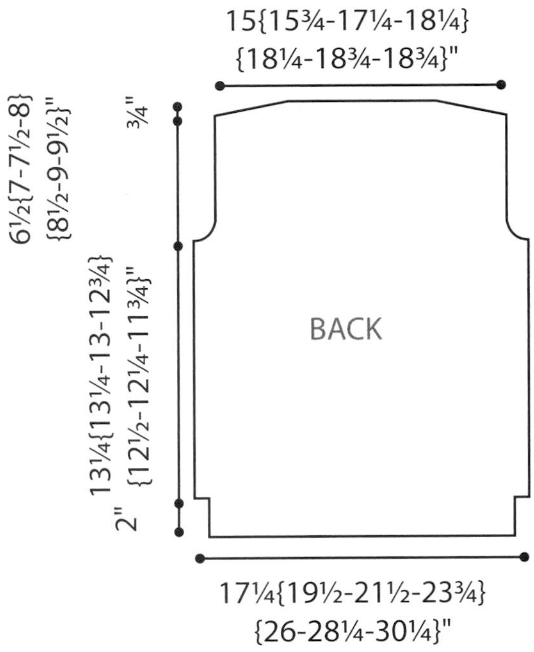
15{15¾-17¼-18¼}
{18¼-18¾-18¾}"
6½{7-7½-8}
{8½-9-9½}"
¾"
13¼{13¼-13-12¾}
{12½-12¼-11¾}"
2"
BACK
17¼{19½-21½-23¾}
{26-28¼-30¼}"

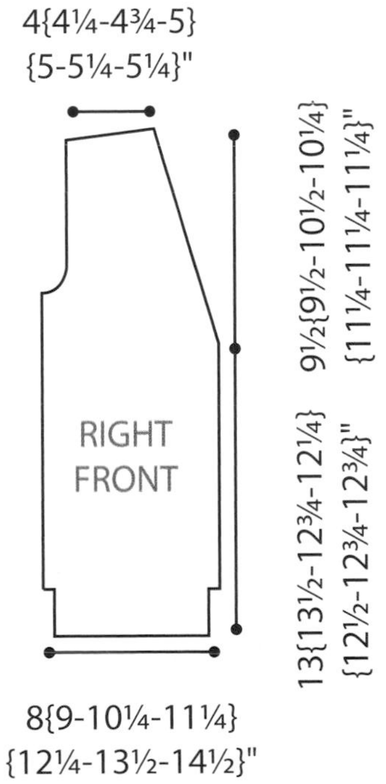
4{4¼-4¾-5}
{5-5¼-5¼}"
RIGHT FRONT
9½{9½-10½-10¼}
{11¼-11¼-11¼}"
13{13½-12¾-12¼}
{12½-12¾-12¾}"
8{9-10¼-11¼}
{12¼-13½-14½}"

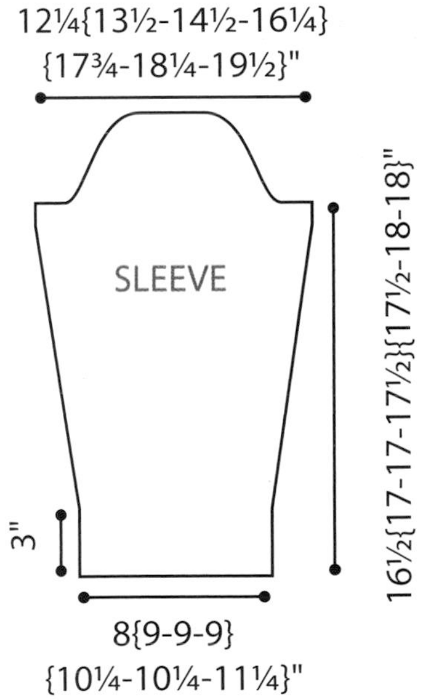
12¼{13½-14½-16¼}
{17¾-18¼-19½}"
SLEEVE
3"
16½{17-17-17½}{17½-18-18}"
8{9-9-9}
{10¼-10¼-11¼}"

Note: Cardigan includes two edge stitches.

PEPLUM PULLOVER

This feminine version of the Zigzag Pullover has a short peplum added to skirt the hips.
This turns the ribbed band into a narrow waist.

▰▰▰▱ INTERMEDIATE

Size	Finished Chest Measurements	
Extra Small	31¾"	(80.5 cm)
Small	35¾"	(91 cm)
Medium	39¾"	(101 cm)
Large	43¾"	(111 cm)
Extra Large	47¾"	(121.5 cm)
2X-Large	51¾"	(131.5 cm)
3X-Large	55¾"	(141.5 cm)

Size Note: Instructions are written for size Extra Small with sizes Small, Medium, and Large in the first set of braces { } and sizes Extra Large, 2X-Large, and 3X-Large in the second set of braces. Instructions will be easier to read if you circle all the numbers pertaining to your size. If only one number is given, it applies to all sizes.

MATERIALS

Light Weight Yarn
[1.75 ounces, 178 yards
(50 grams, 165 meters) per ball]:
  7{8-9-10}{11-12-13} balls
Straight knitting needles,
  sizes 4 (3.5 mm)
  and 5 (3.75 mm) **or**
  sizes needed for gauge
16" (40.5 cm) Circular knitting
  needle, size 4 (3.5 mm)
Stitch holder
Marker
Tapestry needle

GAUGE: With larger size needles, in Body pattern (Simple Texture, page 15), 24 sts and 34 rows = 4" (10 cm)

Techniques used:
- K2 tog (*Fig. 1, page 139*)
- SSK (*Figs. 2a-c, page 140*)
- Slip 1 as if to **purl**, P2 tog, PSSO (*Figs. 3a & b, page 140*)
- Purl Increase (*Fig. 5, page 141*)

BACK
PEPLUM
With larger size needles, cast on 113{129-137-153} {161-177-185} sts.

Row 1: Purl across.

Row 2 (Right side)**:** P1, (K7, P1) across.

Row 3: K2, P5, (K3, P5) across to last 2 sts, K2.

Row 4: P3, K3, (P5, K3) across to last 3 sts, P3.

Row 5: K4, P1, (K7, P1) across to last 4 sts, K4.

Row 6: P4, K1, (P7, K1) across to last 4 sts, P4.

Repeat Rows 5 and 6 until Peplum measures approximately 5" (12.5 cm) from cast on edge, ending by working Row 6.

WAIST SHAPING
Change to smaller size straight needles.

Size Extra Small ONLY
Row 1 (Decrease row)**:** (K1, P1) 3 times, K1, slip 1 as if to **purl**, P2 tog, PSSO, (K1, P1) twice, K1, ★ slip 1 as if to **purl**, P2 tog, PSSO, (K1, P1) 6 times, K1; repeat from ★ 4 times **more**, slip 1 as if to **purl**, P2 tog, PSSO, (K1, P1) twice, K1, slip 1 as if to **purl**, P2 tog, PSSO, (K1, P1) 3 times, K1: 97 sts.

Size Small ONLY
Row 1 (Decrease row)**:** (K1, P1) 3 times, K1, [slip 1 as if to **purl**, P2 tog, PSSO, (K1, P1) twice, K1] twice, ★ slip 1 as if to **purl**, P2 tog, PSSO, (K1, P1) 6 times, K1; repeat from ★ 4 times **more**, [slip 1 as if to **purl**, P2 tog, PSSO, (K1, P1) twice, K1] 3 times, P1, K1: 109 sts.

Size Medium ONLY
Row 1 (Decrease row)**:** (K1, P1) 3 times, K1, [slip 1 as if to **purl**, P2 tog, PSSO, (K1, P1) 6 times, K1] 3 times, slip 1 as if to **purl**, P2 tog, PSSO, (K1, P1) 10 times, K1, [slip 1 as if to **purl**, P2 tog, PSSO, (K1, P1) 6 times, K1] 3 times, slip 1 as if to **purl**, P2 tog, PSSO, (K1, P1) 3 times, K1: 121 sts.

Instructions continued on page 108.

Size Large ONLY

Row 1 (Decrease row)**:** (K1, P1) 3 times, K1, ★ † slip 1 as if to **purl**, P2 tog, PSSO, (K1, P1) 6 times, K1 †; repeat from † to † 3 times **more**, slip 1 as if to **purl**, P2 tog, PSSO, (K1, P1) twice, K1; repeat from ★ once **more**, P1, K1: 133 sts.

Size Extra Large ONLY

Row 1 (Decrease row)**:** (K1, P1) 3 times, K1, slip 1 as if to **purl**, P2 tog, PSSO, (K1, P1) 6 times, K1, slip 1 as if to **purl**, P2 tog, PSSO, (K1, P1) 10 times, K1, slip 1 as if to **purl**, P2 tog, PSSO, (K1, P1) 6 times, K1, slip 1 as if to **purl**, P2 tog, PSSO, (K1, P1) 14 times, K1, slip 1 as if to **purl**, P2 tog, PSSO, (K1, P1) 6 times, K1, slip 1 as if to **purl**, P2 tog, PSSO, (K1, P1) 10 times, K1, slip 1 as if to **purl**, P2 tog, PSSO, (K1, P1) 6 times, K1, slip 1 as if to **purl**, P2 tog, PSSO, (K1, P1) 3 times, K1: 145 sts.

Size 2X-Large ONLY

Row 1 (Decrease row)**:** (K1, P1) 3 times, K1, † slip 1 as if to **purl**, P2 tog, PSSO, (K1, P1) 6 times, K1 †; repeat from † to † 3 times **more**, slip 1 as if to **purl**, P2 tog, PSSO, (K1, P1) 14 times, K1, repeat from † to † 4 times, slip 1 as if to **purl**, P2 tog, PSSO, (K1, P1) 3 times, K1: 157 sts.

Size 3X-Large ONLY

Row 1 (Decrease row)**:** (K1, P1) 3 times, K1, ★ slip 1 as if to **purl**, P2 tog, PSSO, (K1, P1) 10 times, K1; repeat from ★ 6 times **more**, slip 1 as if to **purl**, P2 tog, PSSO, (K1, P1) 3 times, K1: 169 sts.

ALL SIZES

Row 2: P1, (K1, P1) across.

Row 3: K1, (P1, K1) across.

Repeat Rows 2 and 3 until piece measures approximately 8" (20.5 cm) from cast on edge, ending by working Row 3.

BODY

Change to larger size needles.

Row 1 (Right side)**:** Knit across.

Row 2: K1, (P3, K1) across.

Row 3: Knit across.

Row 4: P2, K1, (P3, K1) across to last 2 sts, P2.

Repeat Rows 1-4 for pattern until piece measures approximately 15½{15½-15-15}{14½-14½-14}"/39.5{39.5-38-38}{37-37-35.5} cm from cast on edge, ending by working a **wrong** side row.

ARMHOLE SHAPING

Maintain established pattern throughout.

Rows 1 and 2: Bind off 6{6-6-8}{10-15-18} sts, work across: 85{97-109-117}{125-127-133} sts.

Row 3 (Decrease row)**:** K1, SSK, work across to last 3 sts, K2 tog, K1: 83{95-107-115}{123-125-131} sts.

Row 4: Work across.

Repeat Rows 3 and 4, 0{4-6-7}{9-9-11} times (*see Zeros, page 139*): 83{87-95-101}{105-107-109} sts.

Work even until Armholes measure approximately 6½{7-7½-8}{8½-9-9½}"/16.5{18-19-20.5}{21.5-23-24} cm, ending by working a **wrong** side row.

SHOULDER SHAPING

Rows 1 and 2: Bind off 7{7-8-9}{9-9-10} sts, work across: 69{73-79-83}{87-89-89} sts.

Rows 3 and 4: Bind off 7{8-9-9}{10-10-10} sts, work across: 55{57-61-65}{67-69-69} sts.

Rows 5 and 6: Bind off 8{8-9-10}{10-10-10} sts, work across: 39{41-43-45}{47-49-49} sts.

Slip remaining sts onto st holder.

FRONT

Work same as Back until Armholes measure approximately 3½{4-4½-5}{5½-6-6½}"/9{10-11.5-12.5}{14-15-16.5} cm, ending by working a **wrong** side row: 83{87-95-101}{105-107-109} sts.

NECK SHAPING

Both sides of Neck are worked at the same time, using separate yarn for **each** side.

Row 1: Work across 32{33-36-38}{39-39-40} sts; with second yarn, bind off next 19{21-23-25}{27-29-29} sts, work across: 32{33-36-38}{39-39-40} sts **each** side.

Rows 2-5: Work across; with second yarn, bind off 2 sts, work across: 28{29-32-34}{35-35-36} sts **each** side.

Row 6: Work across; with second yarn, work across.

Row 7 (Decrease row)**:** Work across to within 3 sts of Neck edge, K2 tog, K1; with second yarn, K1, SSK, work across: 27{28-31-33}{34-34-35} sts **each** side.

Rows 8-17: Repeat Rows 6 and 7, 5 times: 22{23-26-28}{29-29-30} sts **each** side.

Work even until Front measures same as Back to shoulders, ending by working a **wrong** side row.

SHOULDER SHAPING
Rows 1 and 2: Bind off 7{7-8-9}{9-9-10} sts, work across: 15{16-18-19}{20-20-20} sts.

Rows 3 and 4: Bind off 7{8-9-9}{10-10-10} sts, work across: 8{8-9-10}{10-10-10} sts.

Row 5: Bind off remaining sts on first side; with second yarn, work across.

Bind off remaining sts.

SLEEVE (Make 2)
PEPLUM
With larger size needles, cast on 57{57-65-65}{73-73-73} sts.

Row 1: Purl across.

Row 2 (Right side)**:** P1, (K7, P1) across.

Row 3: K2, P5, (K3, P5) across to last 2 sts, K2.

Row 4: P3, K3, (P5, K3) across to last 3 sts, P3.

Row 5: K4, P1, (K7, P1) across to last 4 sts, K4.

Row 6: P4, K1, (P7, K1) across to last 4 sts, P4.

Repeat Rows 5 and 6 until Peplum measures approximately 2" (5 cm) from cast on edge, ending by working Row 6.

WRIST SHAPING
Change to smaller size straight needles.

Sizes Extra Small & Small ONLY
Row 1 (Decrease row)**:** (K1, P1) 3 times, K1, ★ slip 1 as if to **purl**, P2 tog, PSSO, (K1, P1) 6 times, K1, slip 1 as if to **purl**, P2 tog, PSSO, (K1, P1) twice, K1; repeat from ★ once more, P1, K1: 49 sts.

Sizes Medium & Large ONLY
Row 1 (Decrease row)**:** (K1, P1) 3 times, K1, ★ slip 1 as if to **purl**, P2 tog, PSSO, (K1, P1) 6 times, K1; repeat from ★ 2 times **more**, slip 1 as if to **purl**, P2 tog, PSSO, (K1, P1) 3 times, K1: 57 sts.

Sizes Extra Large, 2X-Large & 3X-Large ONLY
Row 1 (Decrease row)**:** (K1, P1) 3 times, † K1, slip 1 as if to **purl**, P2 tog, PSSO, (K1, P1) 6 times, K1, slip 1 as if to **purl**, P2 tog, PSSO †, (K1, P1) 10 times, repeat from † to † once, (K1, P1) 3 times, K1: 65 sts.

ALL SIZES
Row 2: P1, (K1, P1) across.

Row 3: K1, (P1, K1) across.

Repeat Rows 2 and 3 until piece measures approximately 3½" (9 cm) from cast on edge, ending by working a **wrong** side row.

BODY
Change to larger size needles.

Row 1 (Right side)**:** Knit across.

Row 2: K1, (P3, K1) across.

Row 3: Knit across.

Row 4: P2, K1, (P3, K1) across to last 2 sts, P2.

Maintaining established pattern (Rows 1-4), increase one stitch at **each** edge, every 10{8-10-8}{8-6-4} rows, 7{9-5-7}{7-14-9} times; then increase every 12{10-12-10}{10-8-6} rows, 4{5-6-7}{7-6-16} times: 71{77-79-85}{93-105-115} sts.

Instructions continued on page 110.

Work even until Sleeve measures approximately 18½{19-19-19½}{19½-20-20}"/47{48.5-48.5-49.5}{49.5-51-51} cm from cast on edge, ending by working a **wrong** side row.

CAP SHAPING
Maintain established pattern throughout.

Rows 1 and 2: Bind off 6{6-6-8}{10-15-18} sts, work across: 59{65-67-69}{73-75-79} sts.

Row 2 (Decrease row): K1, SSK, work across to last 3 sts, K2 tog, K1: 57{63-65-67}{71-73-77} sts.

Row 3: Work across.

Repeat Rows 2 and 3, 13{14-16-16}{19-19-21} times: 31{35-33-35}{33-35-35} sts.

Next 2 Rows: Bind off 4{4-3-3}{2-2-2} sts, work across: 23{27-27-29}{29-31-31} sts.

Last 2 Rows: Bind off 3{4-3-3}{2-2-2} sts, work across: 17{19-21-23}{25-27-27} sts.

Bind off remaining sts.

FINISHING
Sew shoulder seams.

NECK RIBBING
With **right** side facing and using circular needle, slip 39{41-43-45}{47-49-49} from Back st holder onto circular needle and knit across; pick up 27 sts evenly spaced along left Neck edge *(Figs. 7a & b, page 141)*, pick up 19{21-23-25}{27-29-29} sts across Front Neck edge, pick up 27 sts along right front Neck edge; place marker to mark the beginning of the rnd *(see Markers, page 139)*: 112{116-120-124}{128-132-132} sts.

Rnds 1-6: (K1, P1) around.

Bind off all sts **loosely** in ribbing.

Sew Sleeves to sweater, placing center of last row on Sleeve Cap at shoulder seam and matching bound off stitches.

Weave side and underarm in one continuous seam *(Fig. 8, page 141)*.

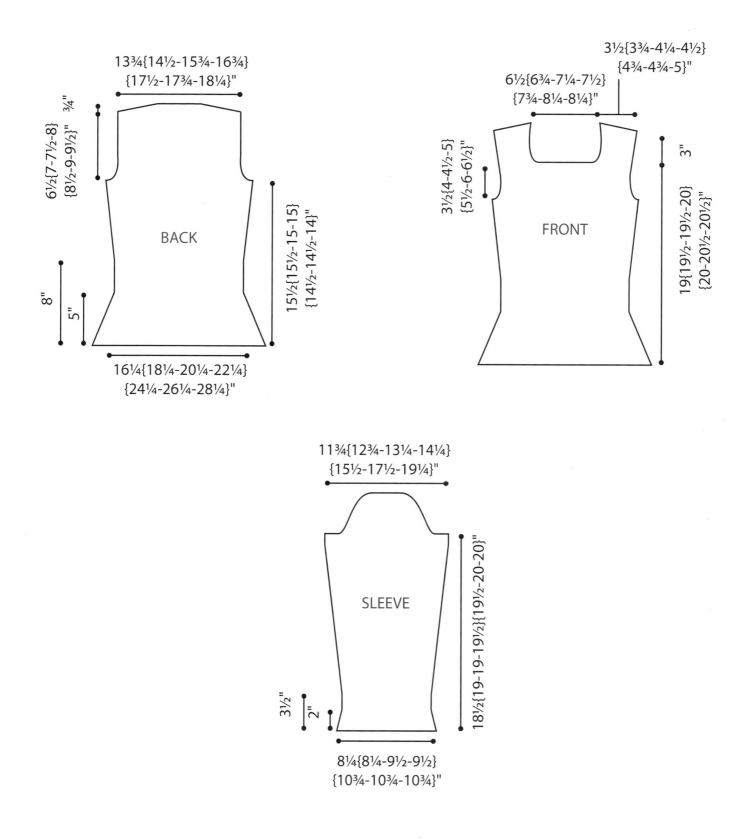

BACK

13¾{14½-15¾-16¾} {17½-17¾-18¼}"

¾"

6½{7-7½-8} {8½-9-9½}"

15½{15½-15-15} {14½-14½-14}"

8"

5"

16¼{18¼-20¼-22¼} {24¼-26¼-28¼}"

FRONT

3½{3¾-4¼-4½} {4¾-4¾-5}"

6½{6¾-7¼-7½} {7¾-8¼-8¼}"

3½{4-4½-5} {5½-6-6½}"

3"

19{19½-19½-20} {20-20½-20½}"

SLEEVE

11¾{12¾-13¼-14¼} {15½-17½-19¼}"

18½{19-19-19½}{19½-20-20}"

3½"

2"

8¼{8¼-9½-9½} {10¾-10¾-10¾}"

Note: Pullover includes two edge stitches.

CROPPED CARDIGAN

One-piece construction enables the use of larger stitch patterns.

■■■□ INTERMEDIATE

Size	Finished Chest Measurement	
Extra Small	34"	(86.5 cm)
Small	37½"	(95.5 cm)
Medium	43"	(109 cm)
Large	46½"	(118 cm)
Extra Large	50¼"	(127.5 cm)
2X-Large	54"	(137 cm)
3X-Large	57½"	(146 cm)

Size Note: Instructions are written for size Extra Small with sizes Small, Medium, and Large in the first set of braces { } and sizes Extra Large, 2X-Large, and 3X-Large in the second set of braces. Instructions will be easier to read if you circle all the numbers pertaining to your size. If only one number is given, it applies to all sizes.

MATERIALS

Medium Weight Yarn (4)
[3.5 ounces, 210 yards (100 grams, 192 meters) per skein]: 5{5-6-7}{7-8-8} skeins
Straight knitting needles, sizes 5 (3.75 mm) **and** 7 (4.5 mm) **or** sizes needed for gauge
29" (73.5 cm) Circular knitting needles, sizes 5 (3.75 mm) **and** 7 (4.5 mm) **or** sizes needed for gauge
Stitch holder
Point protectors - 2
1" (2.5 cm) Buttons - 6
Sewing needle and thread
Yarn needle

GAUGE: With larger size straight needles, in Body pattern (Moss Diamonds, page 36), 22 sts and 28 rows = 4" (10 cm)

Techniques used:
- K2 tog (*Fig. 1, page 139*)
- SSK (*Figs. 2a-c, page 140*)
- Knit increase (*Figs. 4a & b, page 140*)
- Adding New Stitches (*Figs. 6a & b, page 141*)

Cardigan is worked in one piece to underarm.
The stitches are divided and Left Front, Back, and Right Front are worked separately.

BODY
BAND

With smaller size circular needle, cast on 179{199-229-249}{269-289-309} sts.

Row 1 (Right side): K2, P1, (K1, P1) across to last 2 sts, K2.

Row 2: P2, K1, (P1, K1) across to last 2 sts, P2.

Row 3: K1, (P1, K1) across.

Row 4: P1, (K1, P1) across.

Rows 5-12: Repeat Rows 1-4 twice.

Instructions continued on page 114.

BODY
Change to larger size circular needle.

Row 1 (Right side)**:** K4, P1, K3, P1, K1, ★ (P1, K3) twice, P1, K1; repeat from ★ across to last 9 sts, P1, K3, P1, K4.

Row 2: P4, K1, P3, K1, P1, ★ (K1, P3) twice, K1, P1; repeat from ★ across to last 9 sts, K1, P3, K1, P4.

Row 3: K3, P1, K1, ★ (P1, K3) twice, P1, K1; repeat from ★ across to last 4 sts, P1, K3.

Row 4: P3, K1, P1, ★ (K1, P3) twice, K1, P1; repeat from ★ across to last 4 sts, K1, P3.

Row 5: K2, P1, (K1, P1) twice, ★ (K2, P1) twice, (K1, P1) twice; repeat from ★ across to last 2 sts, K2.

Row 6: P2, (K1, P1) twice, ★ (K1, P2) twice, (K1, P1) twice; repeat from ★ across to last 3 sts, K1, P2.

Rows 7 and 8: Repeat Rows 3 and 4.

Rows 9 and 10: Repeat Rows 1 and 2.

Row 11: K4, P1, K2, P1, (K1, P1) twice, ★ (K2, P1) twice, (K1, P1) twice; repeat from ★ across to last 7 sts, K2, P1, K4.

Row 12: P4, K1, P2, K1, (P1, K1) twice, ★ (P2, K1) twice, (P1, K1) twice; repeat from ★ across to last 7 sts, P2, K1, P4.

Repeat Rows 1-12 for pattern until Body measures approximately 10{10-10-9½} {9-9-8½}"/25.5{25.5-25.5-24} {23-23-21.5} cm from cast on edge, ending by working a **wrong** side row.

Dividing Row: Maintaining established pattern, work across first 38{43-50-53}{56-59-61} sts (Right Front), bind off next 10{10-12-16}{20-24-30} sts (Armhole), work across next 82{92-104-110}{116-122-126} (Back), bind off next 10{10-12-16} {20-24-30} sts (Armhole), work across (Left Front).

LEFT FRONT
Maintain established pattern throughout.

With larger size straight needles, work across 38{43-50-53} {56-59-61} sts of Left Front, leave remaining sts on circular needle, placing point protectors on each end to keep sts from slipping off needle while working Left Front.

ARMHOLE SHAPING
Row 1 (Decrease row)**:** K1, SSK, work across: 37{42-49-52} {55-58-60} sts.

Row 2: Work across.

Repeat Rows 1 and 2, 2{4-6-7} {9-11-13} times: 35{38-43-45} {46-47-47} sts.

Work even until Armhole measures approximately 3½{4-4½-5} {5½-6-6½}"/9{10-11.5-12.5} {14-15-16.5} cm, ending by working a **right** side row.

NECK SHAPING
Row 1: Bind off 6{7-9-10} {11-12-12} sts, work across: 29{31-34-35}{35-35-35} sts.

Row 2 (Decrease row)**:** Work across to last 3 sts, K2 tog, K1: 28{30-33-34} {34-34-34} sts.

Row 3: Work across.

Rows 4-17: Repeat Rows 2 and 3, 7 times: 21{23-26-27}{27-27-27} sts.

Work even until Armhole measures approximately 6½{7-7½-8} {8½-9-9½}"/16.5{18-19-20.5} {21.5-23-24} cm, ending by working a **wrong** side row.

SHOULDER SHAPING
Row 1: Bind off 7{7-8-9}{9-9-9} sts, work across: 14{16-18-18} {18-18-18} sts.

Row 2: Work across.

Row 3: Bind off 7{8-9-9}{9-9-9} sts, work across: 7{8-9-9}{9-9-9} sts.

Row 4: Work across.

Bind off remaining sts.

BACK
Maintain established pattern throughout.

With **wrong** side facing and using larger size straight needles, work across next 83{93-105-111} {117-123-127} sts of Back, leave remaining sts on circular needle, placing point protectors on each end to keep sts from slipping off needle while working Back.

ARMHOLE SHAPING

Row 1 (Decrease row)**:** K1, SSK, work across to last 3 sts, K2 tog, K1: 81{91-103-109}{115-121-125} sts.

Row 2: Work across.

Repeat Rows 1 and 2, 2{4-6-7}{9-11-13} times: 77{83-91-95}{97-99-99} sts.

Work even until Armholes measure same as Left Front to shoulder, ending by working a **wrong** side row.

SHOULDER SHAPING

Rows 1 and 2: Bind off 7{7-8-9}{9-9-9} sts, work across: 63{69-75-77}{79-81-81} sts.

Rows 3-6: Bind off 7{8-9-9}{9-9-9} sts, work across: 35{37-39-41}{43-45-45} sts.

Slip remaining sts onto st holder.

RIGHT FRONT
Maintain established pattern throughout.

With **wrong** side facing and using larger size straight needles, work across: 38{43-50-53}{56-59-61} sts.

ARMHOLE SHAPING

Row 1 (Decrease row)**:** Work across to last 3 sts, K2 tog, K1: 37{42-49-52}{55-58-60} sts.

Row 2: Work across.

Repeat Rows 1 and 2, 2{4-6-7}{9-11-13} times: 35{38-43-45}{46-47-47} sts.

Work even until Armhole measures same as Left Front to Neck Shaping, ending by working a **wrong** side row.

NECK SHAPING

Row 1: Bind off 6{7-9-10}{11-12-12} sts, work across: 29{31-34-35}{35-35-35} sts.

Row 2: Work across.

Row 3: K1, SSK, work across: 28{30-33-34}{34-34-34) sts.

Rows 4-17: Repeat Rows 2 and 3, 7 times: 21{23-26-27}{27-27-27} sts.

Work even until Armhole measures same as Left Front to shoulder, ending by working a **right** side row.

SHOULDER SHAPING

Row 1: Bind off 7{7-8-9}{9-9-9} sts, work across: 14{16-18-18}{18-18-18} sts.

Row 2: Work across.

Row 3: Bind off 7{8-9-9}{9-9-9} sts, work across: 7{8-9-9}{9-9-9} sts.

Row 4: Work across.

Bind off remaining sts.

SLEEVE (Make 2)
BAND
With smaller size straight needles, cast on 49{49-49-59}{59-69-69} sts.

Row 1 (Right side)**:** K1, (P1, K1) across.

Rows 2 and 3: P1, (K1, P1) across.

Row 4: K1, (P1, K1) across.

Rows 5-12: Repeat Rows 1-4 twice.

BODY
Change to larger size straight needles.

Working in pattern (Rows 1-12 of Body), increase one stitch at **each** edge, every 16{10-6-8}{6-6-6} rows, 6{4-2-4}{9-3-15} times; then increase every 0{12-8-10}{8-8-8} rows (*see Zeros, page 125*), 0{5-11-7}{6-11-2} times: 61{67-75-81}{89-97-103} sts.

Work even until Sleeve measures approximately 16½{17-17-17½}{17½-18-18}"/42{43-43-44.5}{44.5-45.5-45.5} cm from cast on edge, ending by working a **wrong** side row.

CAP SHAPING
Maintain established pattern throughout.

Rows 1 and 2: Bind off 3{5-7-8}{10-12-14} sts, work across: 55{57-61-65}{69-73-75} sts.

Row 3 (Decrease row)**:** K1, SSK, work across to last 3 sts, K2 tog, K1: 53{55-59-63}{67-71-73} sts.

Row 4: Work across.

Repeat Rows 3 and 4, 9{11-11-12}{12-14-15} times: 35{33-37-39}{43-43-43} sts.

Last 4 rows: Bind off 5{4-5-5}{5-5-4} sts, work across: 15{17-17-19}{23-23-27} sts.

Bind off remaining sts in pattern.

Instructions continued on page 116

FINISHING

Sew shoulder seams.

BUTTON BAND

With **right** side facing, using smaller size straight needles, and beginning at Neck Shaping of Left Front, pick up 71{73-75-75}{75-79-79} sts evenly spaced across to bottom corner *(Figs. 7a & b, page 141)*.

Row 1: K1, (P1, K1) across.

Rows 2 and 3: P1, (K1, P1) across.

Rows 4 and 5: K1, (P1, K1) across.

Rows 6-11: Repeat Rows 2-5 once, then repeat Rows 2 and 3 once more.

Bind off all sts in pattern.

BUTTONHOLE BAND

With **right** side facing, using smaller size straight needles, and beginning at bottom edge of Right Front, pick up 71{73-75-75}{75-79-79} sts evenly spaced across to Neck shaping.

Row 1: K1, (P1, K1) across.

Rows 2 and 3: P1, (K1, P1) across.

Row 4: K1, (P1, K1) across.

Row 5 (Buttonhole row begun)**:** (K1, P1) 2{2-3-3}{3-3-3} times, bind off next 3 sts, ★ (K1, P1) 4 times, bind off next 3 sts; repeat from ★ 4 times **more**, K1, (P1, K1) 1{2-2-2}{2-4-4} times.

Row 6 (Buttonhole row completed)**:** (P1, K1) 2{3-3-3}{3-4-4} times, **turn**; add on 3 sts, **turn**; ★ K1, (P1, K1) 4 times, **turn**; add on 3 sts, **turn**; repeat from ★ 4 times **more**, (K1, P1) across.

Beginning with Row 7, complete same as Button Band.

COLLAR

With **wrong** side facing, using smaller size circular needle, and beginning in first st after Button Band, pick up 32{34-35-36}{37-38-38} sts evenly spaced along Left Neck edge to shoulder, P1, (K1, P1) across sts on Back neck st holder, pick up 32{34-35-36}{37-38-38} sts evenly spaced along Right Neck edge to Buttonhole Band: 99{105-109-113}{117-121-121} sts.

Row 1: K1, (P1, K1) across.

Rows 2 and 3: P1, (K1, P1) across.

Rows 4 and 5: K1, (P1, K1) across.

Rows 6-19: Repeat Rows 2-5, 3 times; then repeat Rows 2 and 3 once **more**.

Bind off all sts **loosely** in pattern.

Sew Sleeves to sweater, placing center of last row on Sleeve Cap at shoulder seam and matching bound off stitches.

Weave underarm seam *(Fig. 8, page 141)*.

Sew buttons to Left Front opposite buttonholes.

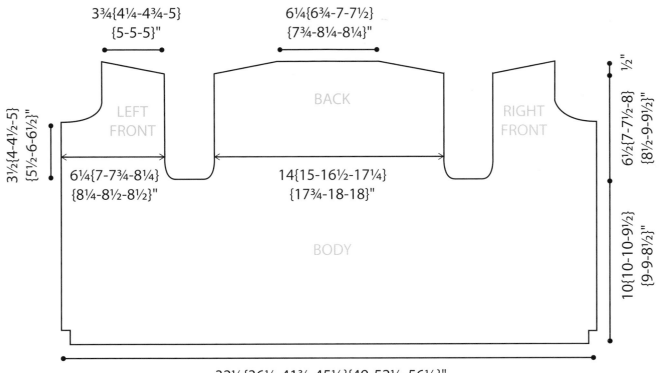

3¾{4¼-4¾-5}
{5-5-5}"

6¼{6¾-7-7½}
{7¾-8¼-8¼}"

½"

LEFT
FRONT

BACK

RIGHT
FRONT

6½{7-7½-8}
{8½-9-9½}"

3½{4-4½-5}
{5½-6-6½}"

6¼{7-7¾-8¼}
{8¼-8½-8½}"

14{15-16½-17¼}
{17¾-18-18}"

BODY

10{10-10-9½}
{9-9-8½}"

32½{36¼-41¾-45¼}{49-52½-56¼}"

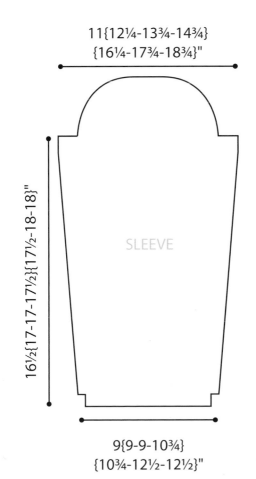

11{12¼-13¾-14¾}
{16¼-17¾-18¾}"

SLEEVE

16½{17-17-17½}{17½-18-18}"

Note: Cardigan includes
two edge stitches.

9{9-9-10¾}
{10¾-12½-12½}"

V-NECK VEST

This vest can be casual or dressy, depending on the buttons you choose.
The front border and buttonhole band are worked as you go!

◼◼◼◻ INTERMEDIATE

Size	Finished Chest Measurement	
Extra Small	34¾"	(88.5 cm)
Small	38¾"	(98.5 cm)
Medium	43"	(109 cm)
Large	46¾"	(119 cm)
Extra Large	51¼"	(130 cm)
2X-Large	55¼ "	(140.5 cm)
3X-Large	59¾"	(152 cm)

Size Note: Instructions are written for size Extra Small with sizes Small, Medium, and Large in the first set of braces { } and sizes Extra Large, 2X-Large, and 3X-Large in the second set of braces. Instructions will be easier to read if you circle all the numbers pertaining to your size. If only one number is given, it applies to all sizes.

MATERIALS

MEDIUM 4

Medium Weight Yarn
[3.5 ounces, 210 yards (100 grams, 192 meters) per skein]: 3{3-4-4}{5-5-6} skeins
Straight knitting needles, sizes 5 (3.75 mm) **and** 7 (4.5 mm) **or** sizes needed for gauge
16" (40.5 cm) Circular knitting needle, size 5 (3.75 mm)
Markers
Yarn needle
Sewing needle and thread
⅝" (16 mm) Buttons - 5

GAUGE: With larger size needles, in Body pattern (Diamond Panels, page 28), 24 sts = 5" (12.75 cm); 32 rows = 4" (10 cm)

Techniques used:
• K2 tog *(Fig. 1, page 139)*
• SSK *(Figs. 2a-c, page 141)*

BACK
BOTTOM BORDER

With smaller size straight needles, cast on 85{95-105-115}{125-135-145} sts.

Rows 1-11: P1, (K1, P1) across.

BODY
Change to larger size needles.

Row 1 (Right side)**:** K2{3-4-1}{2-3-4}, place marker *(see Markers, page 139)*, knit across to last 2{3-4-1}{2-3-4} sts, place marker, K2{3-4-1}{2-3-4}.

Row 2: Purl across to marker, K1, (P7, K1) across to next marker, purl across.

Row 3: Knit across to marker, K4, P1, (K7, P1) across to within 4 sts of next marker, knit across.

Row 4: Purl across to marker, K1, (P2, K1, P1, K1, P2, K1) across to next marker, purl across.

Row 5: Knit across to marker, K2, P1, (K1, P1) twice, ★ K3, P1, (K1, P1) twice; repeat from ★ across to within 2 sts of next marker, knit across.

Instructions continued on page 120.

Row 6: Purl across to marker, K1, (P2, K1, P1, K1, P2, K1) across to next marker, purl across.

Row 7: Knit across to marker, (K4, P1, K3) across to within one st of next marker, knit across.

Row 8: Purl across to marker, K1, (P7, K1) across to next marker, purl across.

Repeat Rows 1-8 for pattern until Back measures approximately 11½" (29 cm) from cast on edge, ending by working a **wrong** side row.

ARMHOLE SHAPING
Maintain established pattern throughout.

Rows 1 and 2: Bind off 5{7-7-9} {10-12-15} sts, work across: 75{81-91-97}{105-111-115} sts.

Row 3 (Decrease row)**:** K1, SSK, work across to last 3 sts, K2 tog, K1: 73{79-89-95}{103-109-113} sts.

Row 4: Work across.

Repeat Rows 3 and 4, 4{5-7-7} {10-12-14} times: 65{69-75-81} {83-85-85} sts.

Work even until Armholes measure approximately 6¾{7¼-7¾-8¼} {8¾-9¼-9¾}"/17{18.5-19.5-21} {22-23.5-25} cm, ending by working a **wrong** side row.

SHOULDER SHAPING
Rows 1 and 2: Bind off 6{6-8-9} {9-9-9} sts, work across: 53{57-59-63}{65-67-67} sts.

Rows 3 and 4: Bind off 6{6-8-9} {10-10-10} sts, work across: 41{45-43-45}{45-47-47} sts.

Bind off remaining sts in pattern.

LEFT FRONT
BOTTOM BORDER
With smaller size straight needles, cast on 47{51-57-61}{67-71-77} sts.

Rows 1-11: K1, (P1, K1) across.

BODY
Change to larger size needles.

Row 1 (Right side)**:** K6{2-0-4}{2-6-4} *(see Zeros, page 139)*, place marker, knit across to last 7 sts, place marker, K1, (P1, K1) across (Band).

Row 2: K1, (P1, K1) across to marker, P1, K1, (P7, K1) across to next marker, purl across.

Row 3: Knit across to marker, K4, P1, (K7, P1) across to within 5 sts of next marker, K6, (P1, K1) across.

Row 4: K1, (P1, K1) across to marker, P1, K1, P2, K1, P1, K1, ★ (P2, K1) twice, P1, K1; repeat from ★ across to within 3 sts of next marker, P2, K1, purl across.

Row 5: Knit across to marker, K2, ★ P1, (K1, P1) twice, K3; repeat from ★ across to next marker, K1, (P1, K1) across.

Row 6: K1, (P1, K1) across to marker, P1, K1, P2, K1, ★ P1, K1, (P2, K1) twice; repeat from ★ across to within 5 sts of next marker, P1, K1, P2, K1, purl across.

Row 7: Knit across to marker, K4, P1, (K7, P1) across to within 5 sts of next marker, K6, (P1, K1) across.

Row 8: K1, (P1, K1) across to marker, P1, K1, (K7, P1) across to next marker, purl across.

Row 9: Knit across to second marker, K1, (P1, K1) across.

Rows 10-64: Repeat Rows 2-9, 6 times; then repeat Rows 2-8 once **more**.

NECK & ARMHOLE SHAPING
Row 1 (Decrease row)**:** Knit across to within 2 sts of second marker, K2 tog, K1, (P1, K1) across: 46{50-56-60}{66-70-76} sts.

Maintaining established pattern throughout, continue to decrease every fourth row at Neck edge in same manner, 16{17-17-17} {18-18-19} times AND AT THE SAME TIME when Left Front measures 11½" (29 cm) from cast on edge, ending by working a **wrong** side row, work Armhole Shaping as follows: Bind off 5{7-7-9} {10-12-15} sts at beginning of next row, then K1, SSK at armhole edge on next 5{6-8-8}{11-13-15} **right** side rows: 20{20-24-26}{27-27-27} sts.

Work even until Left Front measures same as Back to shoulder, ending by working a **wrong** side row.

SHOULDER SHAPING
Row 1: Bind off 6{6-8-9}{9-9-9} sts, work across: 14{14-16-17} {18-18-18} sts.

Row 2: Work across.

Row 3: Bind off 6{6-8-9} {10-10-10} sts, work across: 8 sts.

BACK NECK BAND

Row 1: (K1, P1) across.

Row 2: (P1, K1) across.

Repeat Rows 1 and 2 until Back Neck Band measures approximately 4{4½-4¼-4½}{4½-4¾-4¾}"/ 10{11.5-11-11.5}{11.5-12-12} cm, ending by working Row 1.

Bind off all sts in pattern.

RIGHT FRONT
BOTTOM BORDER

With smaller size straight needles, cast on 47{51-57-61}{67-71-77} sts.

Rows 1-11: K1, (P1, K1) across.

BODY
Change to larger size needles.

Row 1 (Right side-Buttonhole row): K1, P1, K1, [YO, K2 tog (**Buttonhole made**)], P1, K1 (Band), place marker, knit across to last 6{2-0-4}{2-6-4} sts, place marker, knit across.

Row 2: Purl across to next marker, K1, (P7, K1) across to within one st of next marker, (P1, K1) across.

Row 3: K1, (P1, K1) across to marker, K5, P1, (K7, P1) across to within 4 sts of next marker, knit across.

Row 4: Purl across to marker, K1, P2, K1, P1, K1, ★ (P2, K1) twice, P1, K1; repeat from ★ across to within 4 sts of next marker, P2, K1, (P1, K1) across.

Row 5: K1, (P1, K1) across to marker, ★ K3, P1, (K1, P1) twice; repeat from ★ across to within 2 sts of next marker, knit across.

Row 6: Purl across to marker, K1, P2, K1, P1, K1, ★ (P2, K1) twice, P1, K1; repeat from ★ across to within 4 sts of next marker, P2, K1, (P1, K1) across.

Row 7: K1, (P1, K1) across to marker, K5, P1, (K7, P1) across to within 4 sts of next marker, knit across.

Row 8: Purl across to marker, K1, (P7, K1) across to within one st of next marker, (P1, K1) across.

Row 9: K1, (P1, K1) across to marker, knit across.

Rows 10-16: Repeat Rows 2-8.

Row 17 (Buttonhole row): K1, P1, K1, [YO, K2 tog (**Buttonhole made**)], P1, K1, knit across.

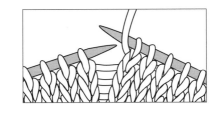

Rows 18-64: Repeat Rows 2-17 twice, then repeat Rows 2-16 once **more**.

NECK & ARMHOLE SHAPING
Row 1 (Decrease and Buttonhole row): K1, P1, K1, [YO, K2 tog (**Buttonhole made**)], P1, K1, SSK, knit across: 46{50-56-60}{66-70-76} sts.

Maintaining established pattern throughout, continue to decrease every fourth row at Neck edge in same manner, 16{17-17-17} {18-18-19} times AND AT THE SAME TIME when Right Front measures 11½" (29 cm) from cast on edge, ending by working a **right** side row; work Armhole Shaping as follows: Bind off 5{7-7-9}{10-12-15} sts at beginning of next row, then K2 tog, K1 at armhole edge on next 5{6-8-8}{11-13-15} **right** side rows: 20{20-24-26}{27-27-27} sts.

Work even until Right Front measures same as Back to shoulder, ending by working a **right** side row.

SHOULDER SHAPING
Row 1: Bind off 6{6-8-9}{9-9-9} sts, work across: 14{14-16-17} {18-18-18} sts.

Row 2: Work across.

Row 3: Bind off 6{6-8-9} {10-10-10} sts, work across: 8 sts.

BACK NECK BAND
Row 1: (K1, P1) across.

Row 2: (P1, K1) across.

Repeat Rows 1 and 2 until Back Neck Band measures approximately 4{4½-4¼-4½} {4½-4¾-4¾}"/10{11.5-11-11.5} {11.5-12-12} cm, ending by working Row 2.

Bind off all sts in pattern.

Instructions continued on page 122.

FINISHING

Sew shoulder seams.
With last rows of Back Neck Bands together, sew seam.
Sew end of rows on Back Neck Band to bound off edge of Back Neck.

Weave side seams *(Fig. 8, page 141)*.

ARMHOLE EDGING

With **right** side facing, using circular needle, and beginning at underarm, pick up 90{96-104-112} {120-128-136} sts evenly spaced around armhole edge *(Figs. 7a & b, page 141)*; place marker to mark the beginning of the rnd.

Rnd 1: (K1, P1) around.

Rnd 2: (P1, K1) around.

Rnds 3 and 4: Repeat Rnds 1 and 2.

Bind off all sts in pattern.

Repeat for second Armhole.

Sew buttons to Left Front Band, opposite buttonholes.

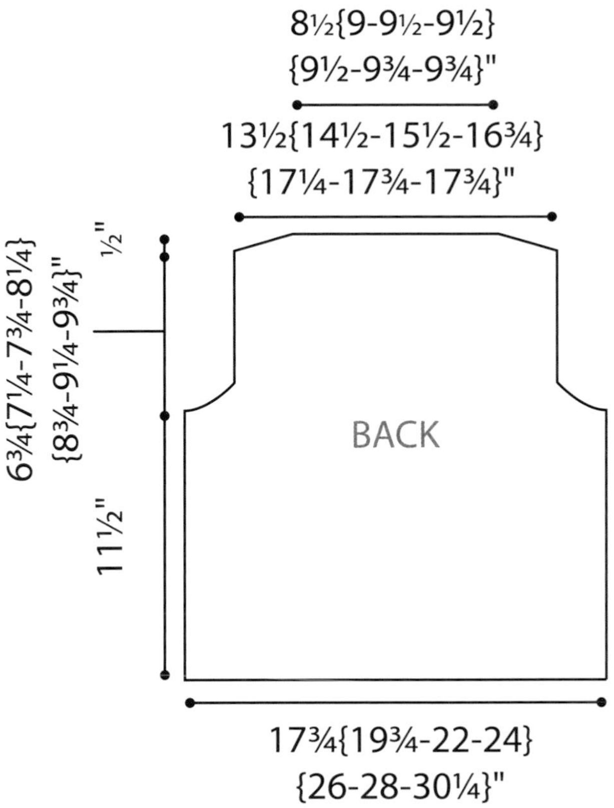
8½{9-9½-9½}
{9½-9¾-9¾}"
13½{14½-15½-16¾}
{17¼-17¾-17¾}"
6¾{7¼-7¾-8¼}
{8¾-9¼-9¾}"
½"
11½"
BACK
17¾{19¾-22-24}
{26-28-30¼}"

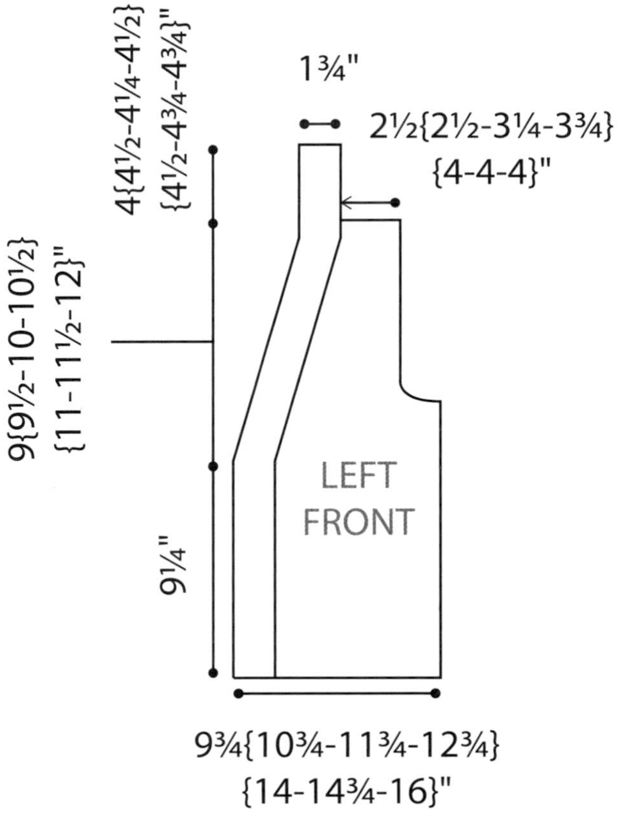
4{4½-4¼-4½}
{4½-4¾-4¾}"
1¾"
2½{2½-3¼-3¾}
{4-4-4}"
9{9½-10-10½}
{11-11½-12}"
9¼"
LEFT
FRONT
9¾{10¾-11¾-12¾}
{14-14¾-16}"

Note: Vest includes two edge stitches.

EMPIRE COAT

The Basket Weave Rib Stitch creates a fresh coat in eight different sizes. Because it's as fun to wear as it is to knit, you may decide to make this jacket again and again.

◖◼◼◼◻ INTERMEDIATE

Size	Finished Chest Measurement	
Extra Small	30¾"	(78 cm)
Small	33½"	(85 cm)
Medium	38½"	(98 cm)
Large	41"	(104 cm)
Extra Large	46¼"	(117.5 cm)
2X-Large	48¾"	(124 cm)
3X-Large	54"	(137 cm)
4X-Large	59"	(150 cm)

Size Note: Instructions are written with sizes Extra Small and Small in the first set of braces { } with sizes Medium, Large, and Extra Large in the second set of braces, and sizes 2X-Large, 3X-Large, and 4X-Large in the third set of braces. Instructions will be easier to read if you circle all the numbers pertaining to your size. If only one number is given, it applies to all sizes.

MATERIALS

LIGHT 3

Light Weight Yarn
[3.5 ounces, 175 yards (100 grams, 160 meters) per hank]:
 {8-9}{10-11-12}{14-15-17} hanks
Straight knitting needles, size 6 (4 mm) **or** size needed for gauge
24" (61 cm) Circular knitting needle, size 5 (3.75 mm)
Stitch holder
¾" (19 mm) Buttons - 5
Sewing needle and thread
Tapestry needle

GAUGE: With straight needles,
 In Garter Stitch Columns (page 35) for bottom of Body,
 21 sts and 32 rows = 4" (10 cm)
 In Basket Weave Rib (page 35) (un-stretched) for top of Body
 25 sts and 32 rows = 4" (10 cm)

Techniques used:
- K2 tog (*Fig. 1, page 139*)
- SSK (*Figs. 2a-c, page 140*)
- Knit increase (*Figs. 4a & b, page 140*)
- Adding New Stitches (*Figs. 6a & b, page 141*)

BACK
BOTTOM BAND

With straight needles, cast on {97-105}{121-129-145} {153-169-185} sts.

Knit 5 rows (Garter Stitch).

BODY

Row 1 (Right side): Knit across.

Row 2: K2, P1, (K3, P1) across to last 2 sts, K2.

Row 3: Knit across.

Row 4: P3, K3, (P5, K3) across to last 3 sts, P3.

Rows 5-9: Repeat Rows 3 and 4 twice, then repeat Row 3 once more.

Instructions continued on page 126.

Rows 10 and 11: Repeat Rows 2 and 3.

Row 12: K2, P5, (K3, P5) across to last 2 sts, K2.

Rows 13-108: Repeat Rows 1-12, 8 times.

Row 109: P1, (K3, P1) across.

Row 110: K1, (P3, K5) across.

Rows 111-114: Repeat Rows 109 and 110 twice.

Row 115: P1, (K3, P1) across.

Row 116: (K5, P3) across to last st, K1.

Rows 117-120: Repeat Rows 115 and 116 twice.

Rows 121-162: Repeat Rows 109-120, 3 times; then repeat Rows 109-114 once **more**.

ARMHOLE SHAPING
Maintain established pattern throughout.

Rows 1 and 2: Bind off {5-6}{8-8-10} {12-14-16} sts, work across: {87-93} {105-113-125}{129-141-153} sts.

Row 3 (Decrease row)**:** K2, SSK, work across to last 4 sts, K2 tog, K2: {85-91}{103-111-123} {127-139-151} sts.

Row 4: Work across.

Repeat Rows 3 and 4, {0-0} {5-4-7}{9-13-19} times *(see Zeros, page 139)*: {85-91}{93-103-109} {109-113-113} sts.

Next {48-52}{46-52-50}{50-46-38} Rows: Work across.

SHOULDER SHAPING
Rows 1 and 2: Bind off {7-8}{8-9-10} {10-10-10} sts, work across: {71-75} {77-85-89}{89-93-93} sts.

Rows 3 and 4: Bind off {7-8} {8-10-10}{10-11-11} sts, work across: {57-59}{61-65-69}{69-71-71} sts.

Rows 5 and 6: Bind off {8-8} {9-10-11}{11-11-11} sts, work across: {41-43}{43-45-47}{47-49-49} sts.

Slip remaining sts onto st holder.

LEFT FRONT
BOTTOM BAND
With straight needles, cast on {53-57}{65-69-77}{81-89-97} sts.

Knit 5 rows.

BODY
Sizes Extra Small, Large, & Extra Large ONLY
Row 1 (Right side)**:** Knit across.

Row 2: K8 (Front Band), P1, (K3, P1) across.

Row 3: Knit across.

Row 4: K8, P5, (K3, P5) across.

Rows 5-9: Repeat Rows 3 and 4 twice, then repeat Row 3 once **more**.

Row 10: K8, P1, (K3, P1) across.

Row 11: Knit across.

Row 12: K8, P1, K3, (P5, K3) across to last st, P1.

Rows 13-108: Repeat Rows 1-12, 8 times.

Row 109: P1, (K3, P1) across to last 8 sts, K8.

Row 110: K9, P3, (K5, P3) across to last st, K1.

Rows 111-114: Repeat Rows 109 and 110 twice.

Row 115: P1, (K3, P1) across to last 8 sts, K8.

Row 116: K 13, (P3, K5) across.

Rows 117-120: Repeat Rows 115 and 116 twice.

Rows 121-162: Repeat Rows 109-120, 3 times; then repeat Rows 109-114 once **more**.

Sizes Small, Medium, 2X-Large, 3X-Large, & 4X-Large ONLY
Row 1 (Right side)**:** Knit across.

Row 2: K8 (Front Band), P1, (K3, P1) across.

Row 3: Knit across.

Row 4: K8, (P5, K3) across to last st, P1.

Rows 5-9: Repeat Rows 3 and 4 twice, then repeat Row 3 once **more**.

Row 10: K8, P1, (K3, P1) across.

Row 11: Knit across.

Row 12: K8, P1, (K3, P5) across.

Rows 13-108: Repeat Rows 1-12, 8 times.

Row 109: P1, (K3, P1) across to last 8 sts, K8.

Row 110: K9, (P3, K5) across.

Rows 111-114: Repeat Rows 109 and 110 twice.

Row 115: P1, (K3, P1) across to last 8 sts, K8.

Row 116: K 13, P3, (K5, P3) across to last st, K1.

Rows 117-120: Repeat Rows 115 and 116 twice.

Rows 121-162: Repeat Rows 109-120, 3 times; then repeat Rows 109-114 once **more**.

ALL SIZES - ARMHOLE SHAPING
Maintain established pattern throughout.

Row 1: Bind off {5-6}{8-8-10} {12-14-16} sts, work across: {48-51} {57-61-67}{69-75-81} sts.

Row 2: Work across.

Row 3 (Decrease row)**:** K2, SSK, work across: {47-50}{56-60-66} {68-74-80} sts.

Repeat Rows 2 and 3, {0-0}{5-4-7} {9-13-19} times: {47-50}{51-56-59} {59-61-61} sts.

Next {28-32}{26-32-30} {30-26-18} Rows: Work across.

NECK & SHOULDER SHAPING
Row 1: Bind off {13-14}{14-15-16} {16-17-17} sts, work across: {34-36} {37-41-43}{43-44-44} sts.

Row 2: Work across.

Row 3: Bind off 2 sts, work across: {32-34}{35-39-41}{41-42-42} sts.

Rows 4 and 5: Repeat Rows 2 and 3: {30-32}{33-37-39}{39-40-40} sts.

Row 6 (Decrease row)**:** Work across to last 3 sts, K2 tog, K1: {29-31} {32-36-38}{38-39-39} sts.

Row 7: Work across.

Rows 8-19: Repeat Rows 6 and 7, 6 times: {23-25}{26-30-32} {32-33-33} sts.

Rows 20-23: Work across.

Row 24: Bind off {7-8}{8-9-10} {10-10-10} sts, work across to last 3 sts, K2 tog, K1: {15-16}{17-20-21} {21-22-22} sts.

Row 25: Work across.

Row 26: Bind off {7-8}{8-10-10} {10-11-11} sts, work across: {8-8} {9-10-11}{11-11-11} sts.

Row 27: Work across.

Bind off remaining sts.

Instructions continued on page 128.

RIGHT FRONT
BOTTOM BAND
With straight needles, cast on {53-57}{65-69-77}{81-89-97} sts.

Knit 5 rows.

BODY
Sizes Extra Small, Large, & Extra Large ONLY
Row 1 (Right side): Knit across.

Row 2: P1, (K3, P1) across to last 8 sts, K8 (Front Band).

Row 3: Knit across.

Row 4: P5, (K3, P5) across to last 8 sts, K8.

Rows 5-9: Repeat Rows 3 and 4 twice, then repeat Row 3 once **more**.

Row 10: P1, (K3, P1) across to last 8 sts, K8.

Row 11: Knit across.

Row 12: P1, K3, (P5, K3) across to last 9 sts, P1, K8.

Rows 13-108: Repeat Rows 1-12, 8 times.

Row 109 (Buttonhole begun): K2, bind off next 2 sts, K3, P1, (K3, P1) across: {51}{67-75} sts.

Row 110 (Buttonhole completed): K1, P3, (K5, P3) across to last 7 sts, K5, **turn**; add on 2 sts, **turn**; K2: {53}{69-77} sts.

Row 111: K8, P1, (K3, P1) across.

Row 112: K1, P3, (K5, P3) across to last 9 sts, K9.

Rows 113 and 114: Repeat Rows 111 and 112.

Row 115: K8, P1, (K3, P1) across.

Row 116: (K5, P3) across to last 13 sts, K 13.

Rows 117-120: Repeat Rows 115 and 116 twice.

Row 121: K8, P1, (K3, P1) across.

Row 122: K1, P3, (K5, P3) across to last 9 sts, K9.

Rows 123-163: Repeat Rows 111-122, 3 times; then repeat Rows 111-115 once **more** AND AT THE SAME TIME work buttonholes every {20}{24-24} rows.

Sizes Small, Medium, 2X-Large, 3X-Large, & 4X-Large ONLY
Row 1 (Right side): Knit across.

Row 2: P1, (K3, P1) across to last 8 sts, K8 (Front Band).

Row 3: Knit across.

Row 4: P1, (K3, P5) across to last 8 sts, K8.

Rows 5-9: Repeat Rows 3 and 4 twice, then repeat Row 3 once **more**.

Row 10: P1, (K3, P1) across to last 8 sts, K8.

Row 11: Knit across.

Row 12: (P5, K3) across to last 9 sts, P1, K8.

Rows 13-108: Repeat Rows 1-12, 8 times.

Row 109 (Buttonhole begun): K2, bind off next 2 sts, K3, P1, (K3, P1) across: {55}{63}{79-87-95} sts.

Row 110 (Buttonhole completed): (K5, P3) across to last 7 sts , K5, **turn**; add on 2 sts, **turn**; K2: {57}{65} {81-89-97} sts.

Row 111: K8, P1, (K3, P1) across.

Row 112: (K5, P3) across to last 9 sts, K9.

Rows 113 and 114: Repeat Rows 111 and 112.

Row 115: K8, P1, (K3, P1) across.

Row 116: K1, P3, (K5, P3) across to last 13 sts, K 13.

Rows 117-120: Repeat Rows 115 and 116 twice.

Row 121: K8, P1, (K3, P1) across.

Row 122: (K5, P3) across to last 9 sts, K9.

Rows 123-163: Repeat Rows 111-122, 3 times; then repeat Rows 111-115 once **more** AND AT THE SAME TIME work buttonholes every {22}{22}{24-26-28} rows.

ALL SIZES - ARMHOLE SHAPING

Maintain established pattern and buttonholes throughout.

Row 1: Bind off {5-6}{8-8-10} {12-14-16} sts, work across: {48-51} {57-61-67}{69-75-81} sts.

Row 2 (Decrease row)**:** Work across to last 4 sts, K2 tog, K2: {47-50} {56-60-66}{68-74-80} sts.

Row 3: Work across.

Repeat Rows 2 and 3, {0-0}{5-4-7} {9-13-19} times: {47-50}{51-56-59} {59-61-61} sts.

Next {28-32}{26-32-30}{30-26-18} Rows: Work across.

NECK & SHOULDER SHAPING

Row 1: Bind off {13-14}{14-15-16} {16-17-17} sts, work across: {34-36} {37-41-43}{43-44-44} sts.

Row 2: Work across.

Row 3: Bind off 2 sts, work across: {32-34}{35-39-41}{41-42-42} sts.

Rows 4 and 5: Repeat Rows 2 and 3: {30-32}{33-37-39}{39-40-40} sts.

Row 6: Work across.

Row 7 (Decrease row)**:** K1, K2 tog, work across: {29-31}{32-36-38} {38-39-39} sts.

Rows 8-19: Repeat Rows 6 and 7, 6 times: {23-25}{26-30-32} {32-33-33} sts.

Rows 20-23: Work across.

Row 24: Bind off {7-8}{8-9-10} {10-10-10} sts, work across to last 3 sts, K2 tog, K1: {15-16}{17-20-21} {21-22-22} sts.

Row 25: Work across.

Row 26: Bind off {7-8}{8-10-10} {10-11-11} sts, work across: {8-8}{9-10-11}{11-11-11} sts.

Row 27: Work across.

Bind off remaining sts.

SLEEVE (Make 2)

Cast on {49-49}{49-57-57} {57-65-65} sts.

Working in Basket Weave Rib pattern (Rows 109-120 of Back Body), increase one stitch at **each** edge, every {12-10}{8-8-6} {4-4-4} rows, {8-8}{16-14-14} {4-4-14} times; then increase every {14-12}{0-10-8}{6-6-6} rows, {2-4} {0-2-6}{20-20-14} times: {69-73} {81-89-97}{105-113-121} sts.

Work even until Sleeve measures approximately {16½-17} {17-17½-17½}{18-18-18½}"/{42-43} {43-44.5-44.5}{45.5-45.5-47} cm from cast on edge, ending by working a **wrong** side row.

CAP SHAPING

Maintain established pattern throughout.

Rows 1 and 2: Bind off {5-6}{8-8-10} {12-14-16} sts, work across: {59-61}{65-73-77}{81-85-89} sts.

Row 3 (Decrease row)**:** K2, SSK, work across to last 4 sts, K2 tog, K1: {57-59}{63-71-75}{79-83-87} sts.

Row 4: Work across.

Repeat Rows 3 and 4, {13-13} {15-15-17}{17-19-21} times: {31-33} {33-41-41}{45-45-45} sts.

Last 4 Rows: Bind off 4 sts, work across: {15-17}{17-25-25} {29-29-29} sts.

Bind off remaining sts.

Instructions continued on page 130.

FINISHING

Sew shoulder seams.

COLLAR

With **wrong** side facing, using circular needle, and beginning in first st after Front Band; pick up {30-31}{31-32-33}{33-34-34} sts evenly spaced along Left Neck edge (*Figs. 7a & b, page 141*), slip {41-43}{43-45-47}{47-49-49} sts from st holder onto an empty straight needle and knit across, pick up {30-31}{31-32-33}{33-34-34} sts evenly spaced along Right Neck edge ending in last st before Band: {101-105}{105-109-113} {113-117-117} sts.

Row 1: P2, knit across to last 2 sts, P2.

Row 2 (Right side)**:** Knit across.

Rows 3-22: Repeat Rows 1 and 2, 10 times.

Row 23: Purl across.

Bind off all sts **loosely** in **knit**.

Sew Sleeves to sweater, placing center of last row on Sleeve Cap at shoulder seam and matching bound off stitches.

Weave side and underarm in one continuous seam (*Fig. 8, page 141*).

Sew buttons to Left Front Band opposite buttonholes.

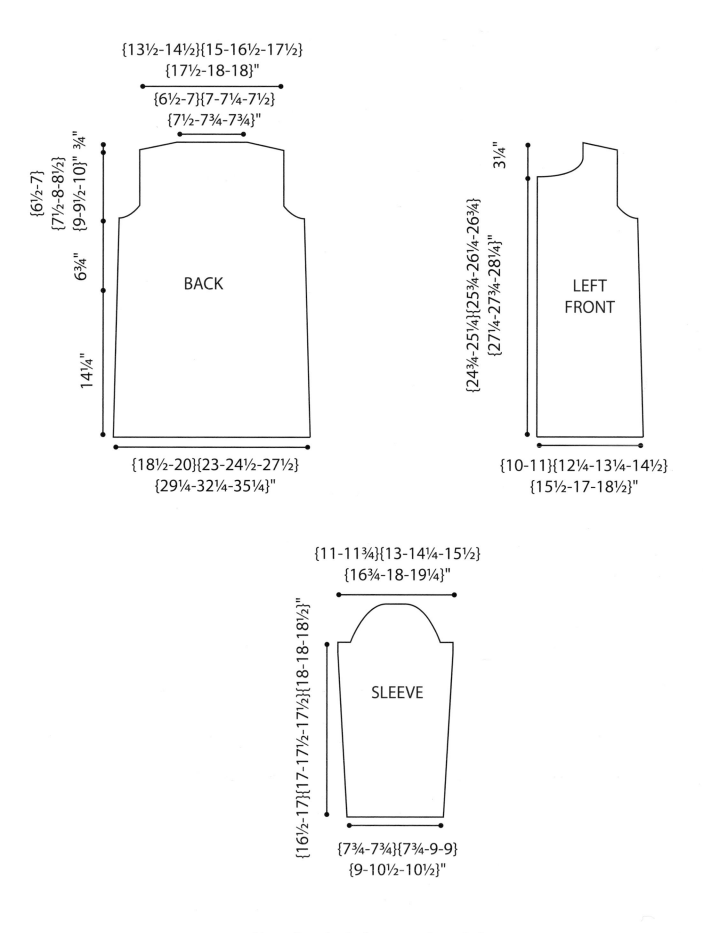

{13½-14½}{15-16½-17½}
{17½-18-18}"

{6½-7}{7-7¼-7½}
{7½-7¾-7¾}"

¾"

{6½-7}
{7½-8-8½}
{9-9½-10}"

6¾"

14¼"

BACK

3¼"

{24¾-25¼}{25¾-26¼-26¾}
{27¼-27¾-28¼}"

LEFT
FRONT

{18½-20}{23-24½-27½}
{29¼-32¼-35¼}"

{10-11}{12¼-13¼-14½}
{15½-17-18½}"

{11-11¾}{13-14¼-15½}
{16¾-18-19¼}"

{16½-17}{17-17½-17½}{18-18-18½}"

SLEEVE

{7¾-7¾}{7¾-9-9}
{9-10½-10½}"

Note: Coat includes two edge stitches.

GIRLS' DIAMOND TUNIC

This girls' sweater is tunic length—6" (15 cm) below waist—and sized with room to grow.

■■■□ INTERMEDIATE

Size	Finished Chest Measurement	
6	28¼"	(72 cm)
8	30¼"	(77 cm)
10	32¼"	(82 cm)
12	34¼"	(87 cm)
14	37"	(94 cm)

Size Note: Instructions are written with sizes 6 and 8 in the first set of braces { } and sizes 10, 12, and 14 in the second set of braces. Instructions will be easier to read if you circle all the numbers pertaining to your size. If only one number is given, it applies to all sizes.

MATERIALS

Light Weight Yarn
[3 ounces, 279 yards
(85 grams, 255 meters) per ball]:
    {4-5}{6-7-8} balls
Straight knitting needles,
    size 5 (3.75 mm) **or**
    size needed for gauge
16" (40.5 cm) Circular knitting
    needle, size 5 (3.75 mm)
Marker
Tapestry needle

GAUGE: With larger size needles, in pattern stitches (Rib and Diamond, page 38 and Ladder, page 22), 24 sts and 33 rows = 4" (10 cm)

Techniques used:
• K2 tog *(Fig. 1, page 139)*
• SSK *(Figs. 2a-c, page 140)*
• Purl Increase *(Fig. 5, page 141)*

BACK
RIBBING

With straight needles, cast on {87-93}{99-105-113} sts.

Row 1: K{2-0}{3-1-0} *(see Zeros, page 139)*, P1, K1, P1, (K2, P1, K1, P1) across to last {2-0}{3-1-0} st(s), K{2-0} {3-1-0}.

Row 2 (Right side): P{2-0}{3-1-0}, K3, (P2, K3) across to last {2-0}{3-1-0} st(s), P{2-0}{3-1-0}.

Repeat Rows 1 and 2 until Ribbing measures approximately 2" (5 cm), ending by working Row 1.

BODY

Row 1 (Right side): P{2-5} {8-11-15}, place marker *(see Markers, page 139)*, (K1, P1) twice, K7, P1, K7, (P1, K1) twice, ★ P1, K5, P1, (K1, P1) twice, K7, P1, K7, (P1, K1) twice; repeat from ★ once **more**, place marker, purl across.

Row 2: Knit across to first marker, P3, K1, P6, K3, P6, K1, P3, ★ K1, P5, K1, P3, K1, P6, K3, P6, K1, P3; repeat from ★ once **more**, knit across.

Instructions continued on page 134.

Row 3: Purl across to first marker, (K1, P1) twice, K5, P5, K5, (P1, K1) twice, ★ P1, K5, P1, (K1, P1) twice, K5, P5, K5, (P1, K1) twice; repeat from ★ once **more**, purl across.

Row 4: Knit across to first marker, P3, K1, P4, K3, P1, K3, P4, K1, P3, ★ K1, P5, K1, P3, K1, P4, K3, P1, K3, P4, K1, P3; repeat from ★ once **more**, knit across.

Row 5: Purl across to first marker, (K1, P1) twice, K3, (P3, K3) twice, (P1, K1) twice, ★ P7, (K1, P1) twice, K3, (P3, K3) twice, (P1, K1) twice; repeat from ★ once **more**, purl across.

Row 6: Knit across to first marker, P3, K1, P2, K3, P5, K3, P2, K1, P3, ★ K7, P3, K1, P2, K3, P5, K3, P2, K1, P3; repeat from ★ once **more**, knit across.

Row 7: Purl across to first marker, K1, (P1, K1) twice, P3, K7, P3, K1, (P1, K1) twice, ★ P1, K5, (P1, K1) 3 times, P3, K7, P3, K1, (P1, K1) twice; repeat from ★ once **more**, purl across.

Row 8: Knit across to first marker, P3, K1, P2, K3, P5, K3, P2, K1, P3, ★ K1, P5, K1, P3, K1, P2, K3, P5, K3, P2, K1, P3; repeat from ★ once **more**, knit across.

Row 9: Purl across to first marker, (K1, P1) twice, K3, (P3, K3) twice, (P1, K1) twice, ★ P1, K5, P1, (K1, P1) twice, K3, (P3, K3) twice, (P1, K1) twice; repeat from ★ once **more**, purl across.

Row 10: Knit across to first marker, P3, K1, P4, K3, P1, K3, P4, K1, P3, ★ K1, P5, K1, P3, K1, P4, K3, P1, K3, P4, K1, P3; repeat from ★ once **more**, knit across.

Row 11: Purl across to first marker, (K1, P1) twice, K5, P5, K5, (P1, K1) twice, ★ P7, (K1, P1) twice, K5, P5, K5, (P1, K1) twice; repeat from ★ once **more**, purl across.

Row 12: Knit across to first marker, P3, K1, P6, K3, P6, K1, P3, ★ K7, P3, K1, P6, K3, P6, K1, P3; repeat from ★ once **more**, knit across.

Row 13: Purl across to first marker, (K1, P1) twice, K7, P1, K7, (P1, K1) twice, ★ P1, K5, P1, (K1, P1) twice, K7, P1, K7, (P1, K1) twice; repeat from ★ once **more**, purl across.

Rows 14 thru {120-132} {144-156-168}: Repeat Rows 2-13, {8-9}{10-11-12} times; then repeat Rows 2-12 once **more**.

Bind off all sts in **knit**.

FRONT
RIBBING
Work same as Back.

BODY
Rows 1 thru {108-120} {132-144-156}: Work same as Back: {87-93}{99-105-113} sts.

NECK SHAPING
Both sides of Neck are worked at same the time, using separate yarn for **each** side. Maintain established pattern throughout.

Row 1: Work across {31-33} {35-37-40} sts; with second yarn, bind off next {25-27}{29-31-33} sts, work across: {31-33}{35-37-40} sts **each** side.

Row 2: Work across; with second yarn, work across.

Row 3 (Decrease row)**:** Work across to within 3 sts of Neck edge, SSK, K1; with second yarn, K1, K2 tog, work across: {30-32}{34-36-39} sts **each** side.

Rows 4-9: Repeat Rows 2 and 3, 3 times: {27-29}{31-33-36} sts **each** side.

Rows 10-12: Work across; with second yarn, work across.

Bind off remaining sts on **each** side.

SLEEVE (Make 2)
Sizes 6 & 8 ONLY
RIBBING
With straight needles, cast on 39 sts.

Row 1: P1, K2, (P1, K1, P1, K2) 7 times, P1.

Row 2: K1, P2, (K3, P2) 7 times, K1.

Repeat Rows 1 and 2 until Ribbing measures approximately 2" (5 cm) from cast on edge, ending by working Row 1.

BODY
Row 1 (Right side)**:** K1, P1, K5, P1, (K1, P1) twice, (K7, P1) twice, (K1, P1) twice, K5, P1, K1.

Row 2: P1, K1, P5, K1, P3, K1, P6, K3, P6, K1, P3, K1, P5, K1, P1.

Row 3: K1, P1, K5, P1, (K1, P1) twice, K5, P5, K5, P1, (K1, P1) twice, K5, P1, K1.

Row 4: P1, K1, P5, K1, P3, K1, P4, K3, P1, K3, P4, K1, P3, K1, P5, K1, P1.

Row 5 (Increase row)**:** Purl increase, P7, (K1, P1) twice, K3, (P3, K3) twice, (P1, K1) twice, P7, purl increase: 41 sts.

Row 6: P2, K7, P3, K1, P2, K3, P5, K3, P2, K1, P3, K7, P2.

Row 7: P1, K1, P1, K5, (P1, K1) 3 times, P3, K7, P3, (K1, P1) 3 times, K5, P1, K1, P1.

Row 8: P2, K1, P5, K1, P3, K1, P2, K3, P5, K3, P2, K1, P3, K1, P5, K1, P2.

Row 9 (Increase row)**:** Purl increase, K1, P1, K5, P1, (K1, P1) twice, K3, (P3, K3) twice, P1, (K1, P1) twice, K5, P1, K1, purl increase: 43 sts.

Row 10: P3, K1, P5, K1, P3, K1, P4, K3, P1, K3, P4, K1, P3, K1, P5, K1, P3.

Row 11: K1, P1, K1, P7, (K1, P1) twice, K5, P5, K5, (P1, K1) twice, P7, K1, P1, K1.

Row 12: P3, K7, P3, K1, P6, K3, P6, K1, P3, K7, P3.

Sizes 10, 12, & 14 ONLY
RIBBING
With straight needles, cast on 43 sts.

Row 1: P1, K1, P1, (K2, P1, K1, P1) 8 times.

Row 2: K3, (P2, K3) 8 times.

Repeat Rows 1 and 2 until Ribbing measures approximately 2" (5 cm) from cast on edge, ending by working Row 1.

BODY
Row 1 (Right side)**:** (K1, P1) twice, K5, P1, (K1, P1) twice, (K7, P1) twice, (K1, P1) twice, K5, (P1, K1) twice.

Row 2: P3, K1, P5, K1, P3, K1, P6, K3, P6, K1, P3, K1, P5, K1, P3.

Row 3: (K1, P1) twice, K5, P1, (K1, P1) twice, K5, P5, K5, P1, (K1, P1) twice, K5, (P1, K1) twice.

Row 4: P3, K1, P5, K1, P3, K1, P4, K3, P1, K3, P4, K1, P3, K1, P5, K1, P3.

Row 5 (Increase row)**:** Purl increase, P1, K1, P7, (K1, P1) twice, K3, (P3, K3) twice, (P1, K1) twice, P7, K1, P1, purl increase: 45 sts.

Row 6: K1, P3, K7, P3, K1, P2, K3, P5, K3, P2, K1, P3, K7, P3, K1.

Row 7: P1, (K1, P1) twice, K5, (P1, K1) 3 times, P3, K7, P3, (K1, P1) 3 times, K5, P1, (K1, P1) twice.

Row 8: K1, P3, K1, P5, K1, P3, K1, P2, K3, P5, K3, P2, K1, P3, K1, P5, K1, P3, K1.

Row 9 (Increase row)**:** Purl increase, (K1, P1) twice, K5, P1, (K1, P1) twice, K3, (P3, K3) twice, P1, (K1, P1) twice, K5, (P1, K1) twice, purl increase: 47 sts.

Instructions continued on page 136.

Row 10: K2, P3, K1, P5, K1, P3, K1, P4, K3, P1, K3, P4, K1, P3, K1, P5, K1, P3, K2.

Row 11: P2, K1, P1, K1, P7, (K1, P1) twice, K5, P5, K5, (P1, K1) twice, P7, K1, P1, K1, P2.

Row 12: K2, P3, K7, P3, K1, P6, K3, P6, K1, P3, K7, P3, K2.

ALL SIZES
Adding new stitches in Reverse Stockinette, increase one stitch at **each** edge, every fourth row, {9-12}{9-12-15} times; then increase every sixth row, {5-5}{9-9-9} times: {71-77}{83-89-95} sts.

Work even until {7-8}{9-10-11} Rib and Diamond pattern are complete, ending by working Row 12.

Bind off all sts.

FINISHING
Sew shoulder seams.

NECK RIBBING
With **right** side facing, using circular needle, and beginning at right shoulder, pick up {33-35}{37-39-41} sts across Back Neck edge *(Figs. 7a & b, page 141)*, pick up {14-14}{12-13-13} sts evenly spaced along left Neck edge, pick up {25-27}{29-31-33} sts across Front Neck edge, pick up {13-14}{12-12-13} sts evenly spaced along right Neck edge; place marker to mark the beginning of the rnd **(see Markers, page 139):** {85-90}{90-95-100} sts.

Rnd 1: (P2, K1, P1, K1) around.

Rnd 2: (P2, K3) around.

Repeat Rnds 1 and 2 until Ribbing measures approximately 1" (2.5 cm).

Bind off all sts **loosely** in ribbing.

Sew Sleeves to sweater, placing center of Sleeve at shoulder seam and beginning {6-6½}{7-7½-8}/{15-16.5}{18-19-20.5} cm down from seam.

Weave side and underarm in one continuous seam *(Fig. 8, page 141)*.

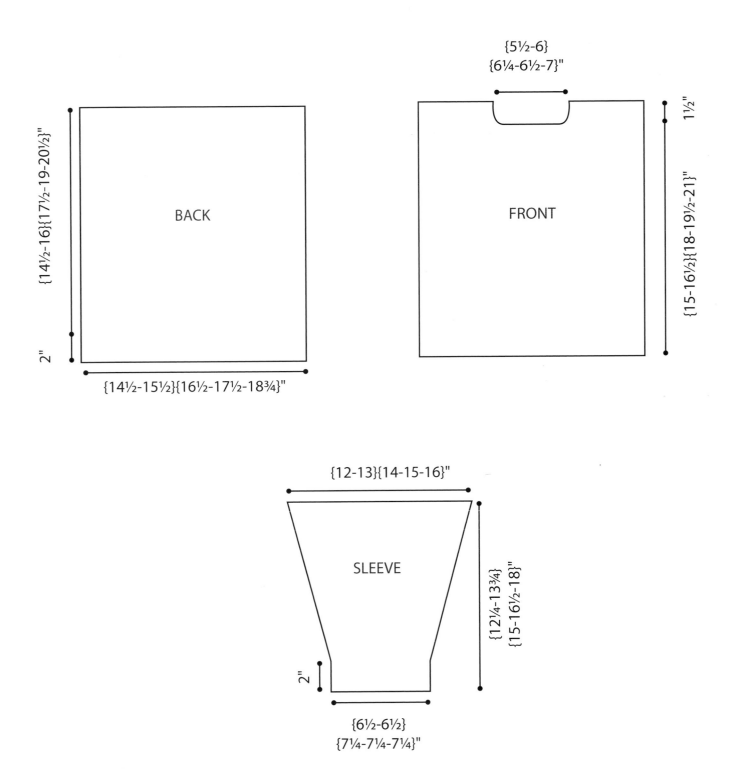

{5½-6}
{6¼-6½-7}"

1½"

{15-16½}{18-19½-21}"

{14½-16}{17½-19-20½}"

2"

BACK

FRONT

{14½-15½}{16½-17½-18¾}"

{12-13}{14-15-16}"

SLEEVE

{12¼-13¾}
{15-16½-18}"

2"

{6½-6½}
{7¼-7¼-7¼}"

Note: Tunic includes two edge stitches.

GENERAL INSTRUCTIONS

ABBREVIATIONS

cm	centimeters
K	knit
mm	millimeters
P	purl
PSSO	pass slipped stitch over
Rnd(s)	Round(s)
SSK	slip, slip, knit
st(s)	stitch(es)
tog	together
YO	yarn over

★ — work instructions following ★ as many **more** times as indicated in addition to the first time.

† to † — work all instructions from first † to second † **as many** times as specified.

( ) or [ ] — work enclosed instructions **as many** times as specified by the number immediately following **or** contains explanatory remarks.

colon (:) — the number(s) given after a colon at the end of a row or round denote(s) the number of stitches you should have on that row or round.

work even — work without increasing or decreasing in the established pattern.

KNIT TERMINOLOGY	
UNITED STATES	**INTERNATIONAL**
gauge =	tension
bind off =	cast off
yarn over (YO) =	yarn forward (yfwd) **or**
	yarn around needle (yrn)

Yarn Weight Symbol & Names	LACE 0	SUPER FINE 1	FINE 2	LIGHT 3	MEDIUM 4	BULKY 5	SUPER BULKY 6
Type of Yarns in Category	Fingering, size 10 crochet thread	Sock, Fingering, Baby	Sport, Baby	DK, Light Worsted	Worsted, Afghan, Aran	Chunky, Craft, Rug	Bulky, Roving
Knit Gauge Range* in Stockinette St to 4" (10 cm)	33-40** sts	27-32 sts	23-26 sts	21-24 sts	16-20 sts	12-15 sts	6-11 sts
Advised Needle Size Range	000-1	1 to 3	3 to 5	5 to 7	7 to 9	9 to 11	11 and larger

*GUIDELINES ONLY: The chart above reflects the most commonly used gauges and needle sizes for specific yarn categories.

** Lace weight yarns are usually knitted on larger needles to create lacy openwork patterns. Accordingly, a gauge range is difficult to determine. Always follow the gauge stated in your pattern.

■□□□ BEGINNER		Projects for first-time knitters using basic knit and purl stitches. Minimal shaping.
■■□□ EASY		Projects using basic stitches, repetitive stitch patterns, simple color changes, and simple shaping and finishing.
■■■□ INTERMEDIATE		Projects with a variety of stitches, such as basic cables and lace, simple intarsia, double-pointed needles and knitting in the round needle techniques, mid-level shaping and finishing.
■■■■ EXPERIENCED		Projects using advanced techniques and stitches, such as short rows, fair isle, more intricate intarsia, cables, lace patterns, and numerous color changes.

KNITTING NEEDLES																			
U.S.	0	1	2	3	4	5	6	7	8	9	10	10½	11	13	15	17	19	35	50
U.K.	13	12	11	10	9	8	7	6	5	4	3	2	1	00	000	---	---	---	---
Metric - mm	2	2.25	2.75	3.25	3.5	3.75	4	4.5	5	5.5	6	6.5	8	9	10	12.75	15	19	25

GAUGE

Exact gauge is **essential** for proper size or fit. Before beginning your project, make the sample swatch given in the individual instructions in the yarn and needle specified. After completing the swatch, measure it, counting your stitches and rows carefully. If your swatch is larger or smaller than specified, **make another, changing needle size to get the correct gauge**. Keep trying until you find the size needles that will give you the specified gauge. Once proper gauge is obtained, measure width of a garment approximately every 3" (7.5 cm) to be sure gauge remains consistent. If you have more rows per inch than specified, use a larger size needle for the purl rows; if fewer, use a smaller size needle for the purl rows.

HINTS

As in all projects, good finishing techniques make a big difference in the quality of the piece. Do not tie knots. Always start a new ball at the beginning of a row, leaving ends long enough to weave in later.
With **wrong** side facing, weave the needle through several stitches, then reverse the direction and weave it back through several stitches. When the ends are secure, clip them off close to the work.

ZEROS

To consolidate the length of an involved pattern, zeros are sometimes used so that all sizes can be combined. For example, every other row, {0-0}{0-0-0}{1-7-5} time(s) means the first 5 sizes would do nothing, the sixth size would increase once, the seventh size would increase 7 times, and the largest size would increase 5 times.

MARKERS

As a convenience to you, we have used markers to help distinguish the beginning of a pattern or round. Place markers as instructed. You may use purchased markers or tie a length of contrasting color yarn around the needle. When you reach a marker on each row or round, slip it from the left needle to the right needle; remove it when no longer needed.

DECREASES
KNIT 2 TOGETHER (abbreviated K2 tog)

Insert the right needle into the **front** of the first two stitches on the left needle as if to **knit** (*Fig. 1*), then **knit** them together as if they were one stitch.

Fig. 1

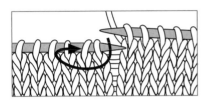

SLIP, SLIP, KNIT (abbreviated SSK)

Separately slip two stitches as if to **knit** (*Fig. 2a*). Insert the **left** needle into the **front** of both slipped stitches (*Fig. 2b*) and then **knit** them together as if they were one stitch (*Fig. 2c*).

Fig. 2a

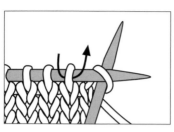

Fig. 2b

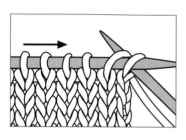

Fig. 2c

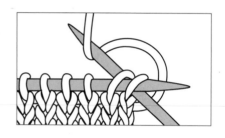

SLIP 1, PURL 2 TOGETHER, PASS SLIPPED STITCH OVER (abbreviated slip 1, P2 tog, PSSO)

Slip one stitch as if to **purl** (*Fig. 3a*), insert the right needle into the **front** of the first two stitches on the left needle as if to **purl** (*Fig. 3b*), then purl them together as if they were one stitch. With the left needle, bring the slipped stitch over the stitch just made (*Fig. 3c*) and off the needle.

Fig. 3a

Fig. 3b

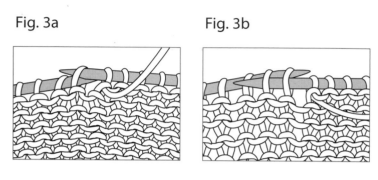

Fig. 3c

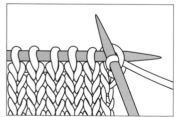

KNIT INCREASE

Knit the next stitch but do **not** slip the old stitch off the left needle (*Fig. 4a*). Insert the right needle into the **back** loop of the **same** stitch and knit it (*Fig. 4b*), then slip the old stitch off the left needle.

Fig. 4a

Fig. 4b

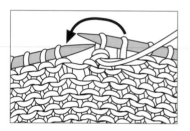

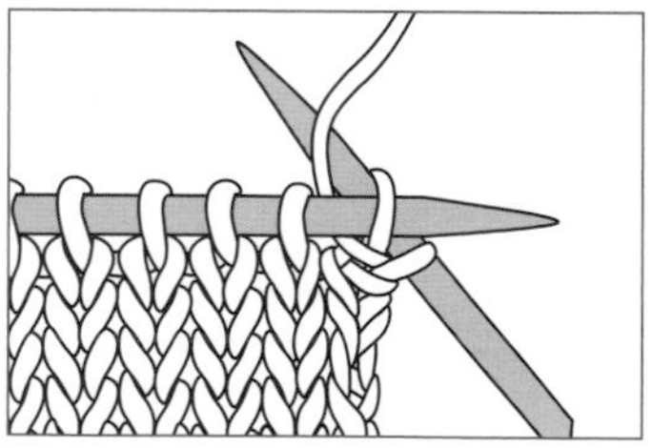

PURL INCREASE

Purl the next stitch but do **not** slip the old stitch off the left needle. Insert the right needle into the **back** loop of the **same** stitch from **back** to **front** (*Fig. 5*) and purl it. Slip the old stitch off the left needle.

Fig. 5

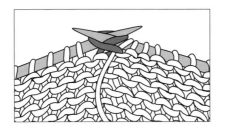

ADDING NEW STITCHES

Insert the right needle into stitch as if to **knit**, yarn over and pull loop through (*Fig. 6a*), insert the left needle into the loop just worked from **front** to **back** and slip the loop onto the left needle (*Fig. 6b*). Repeat for required number of stitches.

Fig. 6a

Fig. 6b

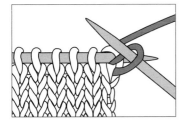
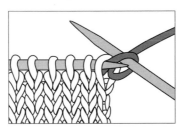

PICKING UP STITCHES

When instructed to pick up stitches, insert the needle from the **front** to the **back** under two strands at the edge of the worked piece (*Figs. 7a & b*). Put the yarn around the needle as if to **knit**, then bring the needle with the yarn back through the stitch to the right side, resulting in a stitch on the needle.

Repeat this along the edge, picking up the required number of stitches.
A crochet hook may be helpful to pull yarn through.

Fig. 7a

Fig. 7b

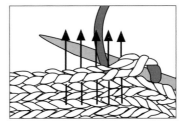
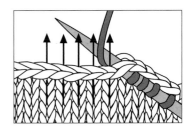

WEAVING SEAMS

With the **right** side of both pieces facing you and edges even, sew through both sides once to secure the seam. Insert the needle under the bar **between** the first and second stitches on the row and pull the yarn through (*Fig. 8*). Insert the needle under the next bar on the second side. Repeat from side to side, being careful to match rows. If the edges are different lengths, it may be necessary to insert the needle under two bars at one edge.

Fig. 8

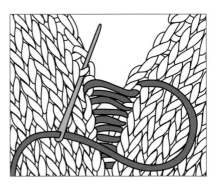

STITCH GALLERY INDEX

YARN INFORMATION

The items in this leaflet were made using a variety of yarns. Any brand of the specified weight of yarn may be used. It is best to refer to the yardage/meters when determining how many balls or skeins to purchase. Remember, to achieve the same look, it is the weight of yarn that is important, not the brand of yarn.

For your convenience, listed below are the specific yarns used to create our photography models.

DISHCLOTHS
Lion Brand® Lion® Cotton
1. Little Pyramid - #133 Paprika
2. Rib and Welt - #134 Avocado
3. Small Basket - #159 Mustard
4. Small Checks - #133 Paprika
5. Knits and Purls - #159 Mustard
6. Moss and Rib Blocks - #134 Avocado

PILLOWS
Lion Brand® Wool-Ease®
1. Garter Diamond - #122 Sienna
2. Tumbling Blocks- #172 Lemongrass
3. Diagonals - #098 Natural Heather
4. Imitation Lattice - #171 Gold
5. Patchwork - #151 Grey Heather
6. Double Basket - #402 Wheat
7. Fancy Track - #403 Mushroom
8. Pinnacle Chevron - #099 Fisherman

SAMPLER THROW
Plymouth Yarn® Encore Worsted
Color A (Ecru) - #1202 White Chocolate
Color B (Purple) - #233 Pastel Purple
Color C (Aran) - #218 Creamy Aran
Color D (Green) - #1231 Pale Green House
Color E (Mint) - #801 Spearmint
Color F (Blue) - #514 Lt Wedgewood
Color G (Beige) - #240 Light Beige Heather
Color H (Dk Beige) - #1415 Dark Beige

GARTER DIAMOND THROW
Patons® Shetland Chunky
#78526 Leaf Green

TUMBLING BLOCKS BABY BLANKET
TLC® Cotton Plus™
#3645 Mint

SUGAR CUBE SHELL
Lion Brand® Microspun
#144 Lilac

WAVY RIB SWEATER
Cascade® Cash Vero DK
#034 Pale Blue

BOY'S CREWNECK PULLOVER
Red Heart® Designer Sport™
#3825 Pool

MEN'S BASKET WEAVE PULLOVER
Lion Brand® Wool-Ease®
Grey - #151 Grey Heather
Red - #138 Cranberry

HIS ZIGZAG PULLOVER
Red Heart® Bamboo Wool
#3525 Peacock

HER ZIGZAG TUNIC
Red Heart® Bamboo Wool
#3265 Gold

LADIES V-NECK CARDIGAN
Berroco® Vintage™
#5192 Chana Dal

PEPLUM PULLOVER
Berroco® Comfort® DK
#2753 Agean Sea

CROPPED CARDIGAN
Patons® Classic Wool
#00240 Leaf Green

V-NECK VEST
Patons® Classic Wool
#77117 Worn Denim

EMPIRE COAT
Louet™ North America Gems
#63 Candy Apple Red

GIRL'S DIAMOND TUNIC
Red Heart® Designer Sport™
#3730 Blush Rose

SPECIAL THANKS

to Noorah
for your patience, your fashion expertise, and your eye for a good button!

to Grandma Willson (1913-2011)
for teaching me to knit

to Marta, Jocelyn, and Aurelia
for cheering me on

to Clay, Calvin, and Dad
for never doubting

to everyone at Leisure Arts
for a dream come true

to the following yarn companies for your generosity

BERROCO, INC
P.O. Box 367
14 Elmdale Road
Uxbridge, MA 05169
(508) 278-2527
www.berroco.com

BROWN SHEEP COMPANY
100662 County Road 16
Mitchell, NE 69357
(800) 826-9136
www.brownsheep.com

CARON INTERNATIONAL
P.O. Box 222
Washington, NC 27889
www.caron.com

CASCADE YARNS
1224 Andover Park East
Tukila, WA 98188
(206) 574-0440
www.cascadeyarns.com

COATS AND CLARK
P.O. Box 12229
Greenville, SC 29612
(800) 648-1479
www.redheart.com
www.coatsandclark.com

LION BRAND YARN CO.
34 West 15th Street
New York, NY 10011
(800) 258-YARN (9276)
www.lionbrand.com

LOUET NORTH AMERICA
3425 Hands Rd
Prescott, ON K0E 1T0
CANADA
(800) 897-6444
www.louet.com

PATONS
320 Livingstone Ave. South
Listowel , ON N4W 3H3
CANADA
www.patonsyarn.com

PLYMOUTH YARN CO.
500 Lafayette St.
Bristol, PA 19007
(215) 788-0459
www.plymouthyarn.com

and to Mama
who would have been so proud,

Couldn't have done it without you!!